Dr Michael M. Gruneberg, designer and writer of the Gruneberg Linkword Language Courses, is widely acknowledged as an international expert on memory improvement. A Senior Lecturer in Psychology at University College, Swansea, he has published a large number of articles in scientific journals, as well as a number of well-known books on the application of memory research. He has also lectured widely in both the UK and the USA and addressed several international scientific conferences. In 1988 he provided the original script for and appeared in *The Magic of Memory*, a programme in the BBC television QED series which illustrated many memory techniques, including his own Linkword Method.

The Linkword Courses have grown out of a large body of published scientific research showing that the imagery method they employ is highly effective in improving the memory for foreign language vocabulary. One study has shown that using this method increases retention from 28% to 88% for a list of 60 Spanish words. Dr Gruneberg has taken this work considerably further, working with linguists and setting out images and testing patterns to create a fully-integrated language-learning system capable of teaching both vocabulary and grammar.

Since it was first published in 1987, the Linkword system has been both highly successful and widely acclaimed.

Language Consultants:
Kyra Veniopoulou and Panicos Georghiades

D1428798

Also by Dr Michael Gruneberg

and published by Corgi Books

LINKWORD
LANGUAGE SYSTEM

GREEK

Dr Michael M. Gruneberg

Language Consultants
**Kyra Veniopoulou and
Panicos Georghiades**

CORGI BOOKS

LINKWORD LANGUAGE SYSTEM – GREEK

A CORGI BOOK 0 552 13907 6

First publication in Great Britain

PRINTING HISTORY
Corgi edition published 1992

This book is set in 9/10 pt Century
by Colset Private Limited, Singapore.

Corgi Books are published by Transworld Publishers
Ltd., 61–63 Uxbridge Road, Ealing, London W5 5SA,
in Australia by Transworld Publishers (Australia)
Pty. Ltd., 15–23 Helles Avenue, Moorebank, NSW
2170, and in New Zealand by Transworld Publishers
(N.Z.) Ltd., 3 William Pickering Drive, Albany,
Auckland.

Made and printed in Great Britain by
Cox & Wyman Ltd., Reading, Berks.

Contents

A Foreword by Paul Daniels

As you may know I, Paul Daniels, am a professional magician, and as such am involved in the business of deception. I am also writing this foreword without ever having seen the full text of this book.

Add these two facts together and you may well wonder why or how I can speak with any degree of authority or expect to be believed when I extol the virtues of the Linkword system.

Well, the simple truth is that one Monday morning at nine a.m. I did not speak a single word of Spanish and by five p.m. on the following Friday I knew hundreds of words of Spanish! I know that is true because I counted them!! Please note the use of the word 'knew' in the last sentence . . . it was chosen deliberately . . . I knew the words positively enough to KNOW that when I said them they were the correct words. My brain reeled with the excitement of learning so much so fast. At forty-eight years of age I had finally got to the stage of being able to communicate with people of another language . . . and how they loved me for trying.

A few weeks later, with no more lessons other than my own reading of Spanish newspapers and books I went on stage and performed my act entirely in Spanish, and now I am 'all fired up' and anxious to learn more. It's wonderful.

Memory systems go back a long way, and I have read many that have suggested their methods could be applied to language learning, but this system is the first I have come across where someone has actually provided a complete system that is 'ready to go'. When you first read memory systems that use idiotic association as a memory aid it is very easy to think that the idea itself is stupid, BUT IT WORKS!!!

So, do yourself a favour and don't knock it till you have tried it. Once you have found out for yourself how to use your own imagination fully to really 'see' the mental images I am sure that like me you will be wondering why this 'game' of learning language is not taught in all our schools.

Paul Daniels

INTRODUCTION

TEST YOURSELF WITH LINKWORD

Picture each of these images in your mind's eye for about ten seconds. For example, the French for *tablecloth* is *nappe*. Imagine yourself having a nap on a tablecloth, as vividly as you can, for about ten seconds.

○ The French for TABLECLOTH is NAPPE
  Imagine having a *NAP* on a *TABLECLOTH*.

○ The German for GENTLEMEN is HERREN
  Imagine a *HERRING* dangling from the door of a
  GENTLEMEN'S toilet.

○ The Italian for FLY is MOSCA.
  Imagine *FLIES* invading *MOSCOW*.

○ The Spanish for SUITCASE is MALETA
  Imagine *MY LETTER* in your *SUITCASE*.

○ The French for HEDGEHOG is HERISSON.
  Imagine your *HAIRY SON* looks like a *HEDGEHOG*.

○ The German for LETTER is BRIEF.
  Imagine a *BRIEF LETTER*.

○ The Italian for DRAWER is CASSETTO.
  Imagine you keep *CASSETTES* in a *DRAWER*.

○ The Spanish for WAITRESS is CAMARERA.
  Imagine a *WAITRESS* with a *CAMERA* slung around her
  neck!

NOW TURN OVER

○ What is the English for CAMARERA? _____

○ What is the English for CASSETTO? _____

○ What is the English for BRIEF? _____

○ What is the English for HERISSON? _____

○ What is the English for MALETA? _____

○ What is the English for MOSCA? _____

○ What is the English for HERREN? _____

○ What is the English for NAPPE? _____

TURN BACK FOR THE ANSWERS

Do not expect to get them all correct at the first attempt. However, if you feel you got more right than you normally would have – then this course will suit you

WHO IS LINKWORD FOR?

The short answer is that Linkword is for anyone and everyone who wants to learn the basics of a language in a hurry. It can be used by children or by adults.

The Linkword Courses have been carefully designed to teach you a basic grammar and words in a simple step-by-step way that anyone can follow. After about 10–12 hours, or even less, you will have a vocabulary of literally hundreds of words and the ability to string these words together to form sentences. The course is ideal, therefore, for the holidaymaker or business person who just wants the basics in a hurry so he or she can be understood, e.g. in the hotel, arriving at the destination, sightseeing, eating out, in emergencies, telling the time and so on.

HOW TO USE LINKWORD

1] You will be presented with words like this:
The Greek for DUCK is PAPYA
Imagine a DUCK wrapped in PAPER.
What you do is to imagine this picture in your mind's eye as vividly as possible.

2] After you have read the image you should think about it in your mind's eye for about 10 seconds before moving on to the next word. If you do not spend enough time thinking about the image it will not stick in your memory as well as it should.

3] After you have been presented with a number of words you will be given a Greek word and asked to give the English.

4] After you have translated from Greek to English you will be asked to translate from English to Greek.

5] When you are asked to translate sentences from English to Greek or Greek to English you can write the answer in.

6] Sometimes the word in Greek and in English is the same or very similar. For example, the Greek for ELEPHANT is ELEFANDAS. When this happens you will be asked to associate the word in some way with a Greek god. For example:
Imagine an elephant trampling on a Greek god.
Whenever a Greek god comes to mind, therefore, you will know the word is the same or similar in both English and Greek.

7] PRONUNCIATION
In this book, you will learn Greek words by being presented with English letters that sound like the Greek word. For example:
The Greek for DUCK is PAPYA.

Representing Greek letter sounds in English presents considerable problems because Greek letters do not always sound like any equivalent in English. For example, in this course the word IS is EENAH. It could equally well be written EENEH or EENE or even INE. Because the first part of the word is stressed, these written forms sound similar when spoken.

Again the Greek letter CHI can sound like the *ch* in lo*ch* or like *hy* (as the sound in *hue*), or like *h* in *h*eater.

4

The Greek letter Γ (GHAMA) is particularly difficult to represent, since there is no equivalent English sound.

In this course rr will represent Γ but the rr sound is very soft, softer than the French r, and made at the back of the throat. It is indistinguishable from a very rough "g" or "gh" sound also made at the back of the throat. Sometimes however, when followed by the letters e and i, the sound of the letter is more like the "y" in "yes".

Because of the difficulty in conveying this letter sound, learners are advised to listen to the audio tape which accompanies this course if they wish to hear the exact pronunciation of words. The pronunciations given in the book are a good approximation, allowing the learner to be understood and to understand when in Greece. However, in order to make the course as easy to learn as possible, we have allowed some slight inconsistencies in the way Greek letters are represented.

8] ACCENTS

In order to help you learn quickly, no accents are given during the course. They are, however, given in the glossary at the end of the course and again the correct pronunciation can be heard on the audio-tape which goes with the course.

Even if you do make a pronunciation mistake, you will almost always be understood, given the context in which you are speaking.

9] LEARNING GREEK LETTERS

At the end of the course, Section 11 teaches you the Greek alphabet, so that you will be able to read as well as to speak Greek. We have deliberately waited until the end of the course to teach the Greek alphabet, as we feel it is important to start learning Greek words as quickly as possible after you open the book. Furthermore, we believe it easier to pick up the Greek alphabet if you know what the word sounds like in English before you are shown how it is written in Greek. The capitals are taught first and then lower case letters are related to the capitals.

While it is best for learning if the learner follows Section 11 as it is laid out, the Greek letters can be learned by skipping over the sentence examples. This might be necessary, for example, where a learner has not finished the course but needs to be able to read Greek place-names and so on.

SOME USEFUL HINTS

1. It is usually best to go through the course as quickly as possible. Many people can get through most of the course in a weekend, especially if they start on Friday evening.

2. Take a break of about 10 minutes between each section, and always *stop* if you feel tired.

3. Don't worry about forgetting a few words, and do not go back to relearn words you have forgotten. Just think of how much you are learning, and try to pick up the forgotten words when it comes to revising.

4. Revise after Section 4, Section 8 and at the end of the course. Then revise the whole course a week later and a month later.

5. Don't worry if you forget some words or grammar after a time. Relearning is extremely fast, and going through the book for a few hours just before you go abroad will quickly get you back to where you were.

6. The course will not give you conversational fluency. You can't expect this until you go abroad and live in a country for a period of time. What it will give you very rapidly is the ability to survive in a large number of situations you will meet abroad. Once you have got this framework, you will find it much easier to pick up more words and grammar when you travel.

IMPORTANT NOTE

The first section of the course can be basically regarded as a training section designed to get you into the Linkword method quickly and easily.

After about 45 minutes you will have a vocabulary of about 30 words and be able to translate sentences. Once you have finished Section 1 you will have the confidence to go through the rest of the course just as quickly. Animal words are used in the first section as they are a large group of "easy to image" words. Many animal words of course are useful to have as they are often met abroad, e.g. dog, cat, etc., or they are edible!

Finally, when it comes to translating sentences the answers are given at the foot of the page. You may find it useful to cover up the answers before you tackle the translations.

VERY IMPORTANT

Greek is one of the more difficult languages for an English speaker to learn. You may have to go through the course in Greek more often than for other languages and you may find your progress slower than for other languages.

Section 1   ANIMALS

THINK OF EACH IMAGE IN YOUR MIND'S EYE FOR ABOUT TEN SECONDS

○ The Greek for CAT is RRATA*
Imagine a RAT And a cat playing together.

○ The Greek for DOG is SKEELOS
Imagine a dog trying to find a SKI LOST on an Alpine slope.

○ The Greek for DUCK is PAPYA
Imagine a duck wrapped in PAPER.

○ The Greek for GOOSE is HYEENA
Imagine a HYEENA killing a big goose.
(N.B. The HY in the Greek word HYEENA is pronounced like the H in HUE).

○ The Greek for HORSE is ALORROH
Imagine taking A LOW ROAD with a horse.

○ The Greek for LOBSTER is ASTAKOS
Imagine you ASKED A CROSS lobster to boil.

○ The Greek for ANIMAL is ZAWOH
Imagine you SAW an old animal in half.

○ The Greek for SALMON is SOLOMOS
Imagine King SOLOMON'S mine full of salmon.

○ The Greek for FISH is PSAREE
Imagine fish wrapped in an Indian SARI.

○ The Greek for WASP is SFEEKA
Imagine a SPEAKER at a dinner being pestered by a wasp.

*Remember a 'RR' in this course is pronounced very softly at the back of the throat – like a very rough 'G'.

YOU CAN WRITE YOUR ANSWERS IN

○ What is the English for SFEEKA?   _____

○ What is the English for PSAREE?   _____

○ What is the English for SOLOMOS?   _____

○ What is the English for ZAWOH?   _____

○ What is the English for ASTAKOS?   _____

○ What is the English for ALORROH?   _____

○ What is the English for HYEENA?   _____

○ What is the English for PAPYA?   _____

○ What is the English for SKEELOS?   _____

○ What is the English for RRATA?   _____

TURN BACK FOR THE ANSWERS

COVER UP THE LEFT HAND PAGE BEFORE
ANSWERING

○ What is the Greek for wasp? _____

○ What is the Greek for fish? _____

○ What is the Greek for salmon? _____

○ What is the Greek for animal? _____

○ What is the Greek for lobster? _____

○ What is the Greek for horse? _____

○ What is the Greek for goose? _____

○ What is the Greek for duck? _____

○ What is the Greek for dog? _____

○ What is the Greek for cat? _____

TURN BACK FOR THE ANSWERS

ELEMENTARY GRAMMAR

GENDERS

In Greek each noun (thing) – whether living or non-living – can be masculine, feminine or neuter.

If the noun is MASCULINE, it usually ends with -OS.

Imagine a MAN falling off an OStrich.

So,

SKEELOS is MASCULINE

If things are FEMININE, they usually end with -A.

Imagine A beautiful little girl.

So,

RRATA is FEMININE

If things are NEUTER, they usually end in -OH or -EE.

Imagine someone saying "OH! and EE!" when they are NEUTERED.

So,

ALORROH is NEUTER
PSAREE is NEUTER

SUMMARY

Gender	Word ending
Masculine	OS
Feminine	A
Neuter	OH or EE

13

Now cover up the answers below, and give the genders of the following:

(You can write your answers in)

1. HYEENA
2. SOLOMOS
3. PSAREE
4. SFEEKA

The answers are:

1. HYEENA is FEMININE
2. SOLOMOS is MASCULINE
3. PSAREE is NEUTER
4. SFEEKA is FEMININE

Although ALL masculine words end with "S", not all of them end with OS. Also, some neuter words end with MA and OS.

Do not worry about these. We will deal with them later.

MORE ANIMALS

THINK OF EACH IMAGE IN YOUR MIND'S EYE FOR ABOUT TEN SECONDS

○ The Greek for JELLYFISH is METHOOSA
Imagine a jellyfish in the water looks like MEDUSA, with her head of snakes.

○ The Greek for FLY is MEEYA
Imagine a fly on a MAYOR's nose.

○ The Greek for HEN is KOTA
Imagine you CAUGHT A hen in a barn yard.

○ The Greek for OCTOPUS is CHTAPOTHEE*
Imagine thinking, "WHAT A PUSSY to catch an octopus."

○ The Greek for INSECT is ENDOMOH
Imagine thinking "This is the END OF MORE insects."

○ The Greek for BEE is MELEESA
Imagine no MALE IS A bee.

○ The Greek for BIRD is POOLEE
Imagine birds caught in a PULLEY.

○ The Greek for WORM is SKOOLEEKEE
Imagine your SCHOOL LEAKY, and worms falling from the roof.

○ The Greek for BUTTERFLY is PETALOOTHA
Imagine you catch a rare butterfly and are told "You'd BETTER LOOSE HER, before the police catch you!"

* Remember that a "CH" in this course is pronounced like the "CH" in a Scottish loch.

YOU CAN WRITE YOUR ANSWERS IN

○ What is the English for PETALOOTHA? _____

○ What is the English for SKOOLEEKEE? _____

○ What is the English for POOLEE? _____

○ What is the English for MELEESA? _____

○ What is the English for ENDOMOH? _____

○ What is the English for CHTAPOTHEE? _____

○ What is the English for KOTA? _____

○ What is the English for MEEYA? _____

○ What is the English for METHOOSA? _____

TURN BACK FOR THE ANSWERS

COVER UP THE LEFT HAND PAGE BEFORE
ANSWERING

○ What is the Greek for butterfly? _____

○ What is the Greek for worm? _____

○ What is the Greek for bird? _____

○ What is the Greek for bee? _____

○ What is the Greek for insect? _____

○ What is the Greek for octopus? _____

○ What is the Greek for hen? _____

○ What is the Greek for fly? _____

○ What is the Greek for jellyfish? _____

TURN BACK FOR THE ANSWERS

ELEMENTARY GRAMMAR

If nouns (things) end in OS they are masculine, like SKEELOS for DOG.

The Greek for THE when the noun is masculine is OH.

So,

    THE DOG   is OH SKEELOS
    THE SALMON is OH SOLOMOS

Try to remember: "OH to hell with HIM!"

The Greek for THE when the noun is feminine is EE.

So,

    THE DUCK is EE PAPYA

Try to remember a little girl saying "HEE HEE".

The Greek for THE when the noun is neuter is TOH.

So,

    The BIRD   is TOH POOLEE
    THE WORM is TOH SKOOLEEKEE
    THE HORSE is TOH ALORROH

Try to remember that the TOE on your foot is neuter.

Now cover up the answers below and translate the following:

(You can write your answers in)

1. THE FLY
2. THE INSECT
3. THE FISH
4. THE DOG

The answers are:

1. EE MEEYA
2. TOH ENDOMOH
3. TOH PSAREE
4. OH SKEELOS

SOME DESCRIPTIVE WORDS

THINK OF EACH IMAGE IN YOUR MIND'S EYE FOR ABOUT TEN SECONDS

○ The Greek for THIN is LEPTOH
Imagine you LEAPT TO help someone who is THIN.

○ The Greek for GOOD is KALOH
Imagine that someone who is CALLOUS is not GOOD.

○ The Greek for BAD is KAKOH
Imagine a BAD man with a nasty CACKLE.

○ The Greek for QUIET is EESEEHOH
Imagine someone EASY GOing and QUIET.

○ The Greek for SMALL is MIKROH
Imagine a SMALL MICRO computer.

YOU CAN WRITE YOUR ANSWERS IN

○ What is the English for MIKROH?   _____

○ What is the English for EESEEHOH?   _____

○ What is the English for KAKOH?   _____

○ What is the English for KALOH?   _____

○ What is the English for LEPTOH?   _____

TURN BACK FOR THE ANSWERS

COVER UP THE LEFT HAND PAGE BEFORE ANSWERING

○ What is the Greek for small? _____

○ What is the Greek for quiet? _____

○ What is the Greek for bad? _____

○ What is the Greek for good? _____

○ What is the Greek for thin? _____

TURN BACK FOR THE ANSWERS

SOME EASY VERBS

THINK OF EACH IMAGE IN YOUR MIND'S EYE FOR ABOUT TEN SECONDS

○ The Greek for IS is EENAH*
  Imagine someone IS IN A temper.

○ The Greek for WAS is EETAN*
  Imagine someone WAS EATEN alive.

* You stress the "EE" part of these words when speaking.

YOU CAN WRITE YOUR ANSWERS IN

○ What is the English for EETAN? _____

○ What is the English for EENAH? _____

TURN BACK FOR THE ANSWERS

26

YOU CAN WRITE YOUR ANSWERS IN

○ What is the Greek for was? _____

○ What is the Greek for is? _____

TURN BACK FOR THE ANSWERS

ELEMENTARY GRAMMAR

You have seen that the Greek word for IS is EENAH.

For example,

    THE DOG IS   is OH SKEELOS EENAH

    THE WASP IS   is EE SFEEKA EENAH

    THE INSECT IS is TOH ENDOMOH EENAH

Adjectives like LEPTOH (thin), KALOH (good), KAKOH (bad), EESEEHOH (quiet), and MIKROH (small) change their endings according to the gender of the noun that they go with.

For example,

    THE DOG IS GOOD   is OH SKEELOS EENAH KALOS

    THE CAT IS GOOD   is EE RRATA EENAH KALEE

    THE HORSE IS GOOD is TOH ALORROH EENAH KALOH

In other words, in the FEMININE and NEUTER, the adjective ends with the same sound as the word for THE.

So,

    THE DUCK IS SMALL is EE PAPYA EENAH MIKREE

    THE FISH IS THIN   is TOH PSAREE EENAH LEPTOH

For MASCULINE words, the adjective ends in the same way as the noun itself.

So,

    THE SALMON IS BAD is OH SOLOMOS EENAH KAKOS

Now cover up the answers below and translate the following:

(You can write your answers in)

1. OH SKEELOS EENAH LEPTOS
2. TOH PSAREE EENAH KAKOH
3. EE HYEENA EENAH MIKREE
4. EE MELEESA EENAH KALEE
5. TOH ALORROH EENAH EESEEHOH

The answers are:

1. THE DOG IS THIN
2. THE FISH IS BAD
3. THE GOOSE IS SMALL
4. THE BEE IS GOOD
5. THE HORSE IS QUIET

Now cover up the answers below and translate the following:

(You can write your answers in)

1. THE BUTTERFLY IS SMALL
2. THE INSECT IS QUIET
3. THE HEN IS GOOD
4. THE DOG IS BAD
5. THE BIRD IS THIN

The answers are:

1. EE PETALOOTHA EENAH MIKREE
2. TOH ENDOMOH EENAH EESEEHOH
3. EE KOTA EENAH KALEE
4. OH SKEELOS EENAH KAKOS
5. TOH POOLEE EENAH LEPTOH

A FEW MORE EASY ANIMALS TO BOOST YOUR VOCABULARY

THINK OF EACH IMAGE IN YOUR MIND'S EYE FOR ABOUT TEN SECONDS

○ The Greek for RABBIT is KOONELEE
  Imagine Sean CONNERY (James Bond) looking like a rabbit.

○ The Greek for DEER is ELAFEE
  Imagine a deer giving A LAUGH EH!

○ The Greek for SNAKE is FEETHEE
  Imagine you FEAR THE snake.

○ The Greek for TORTOISE is HELONA
  Imagine it is HELL ON A tortoise.

○ The Greek for MOSQUITO is KOONOOPEE
  Imagine mosquitoes trying to get through a CANOPY over your bed.

YOU CAN WRITE YOUR ANSWERS IN

○ What is the English for KOONOOPEE? _____

○ What is the English for HELONA? _____

○ What is the English for FEETHEE? _____

○ What is the English for ELAFEE? _____

○ What is the English for KOONELEE? _____

TURN BACK FOR THE ANSWERS

COVER UP THE LEFT HAND PAGE BEFORE
ANSWERING

○ What is the Greek for mosquito?

○ What is the Greek for tortoise?

○ What is the Greek for snake?

○ What is the Greek for deer?

○ What is the Greek for rabbit?

TURN BACK FOR THE ANSWERS

ELEMENTARY GRAMMAR

You have already learnt that the Greek word for WAS is EETAN.

For example,

TOH ELAFEE EETAN is THE DEER WAS

In Greek the adjective (KALOH, LEPTOH, KAKOH, etc.) comes before the noun, as it does in English.

For example,

THE GOOD BEE IS THIN	is	EE KALEE MELEESA EENAH LEPTEE
THE BAD INSECT WAS QUIET	is	TOH KAKOH ENDOMOH EETAN EESEEHOH
THE SMALL LOBSTER WAS THIN	is	OH MIKROS ASTAKOS EETAN LEPTOS

Now cover up the answers below and translate the following:

(You can write your answers in)

1. EE MIKREE MEEYA EENAH KAKEE
2. OH KALOS SKEELOS EENAH LEPTOS
3. EE KAKEE KOTA EETAN EESEEHEE
4. TOH KALOH KOONELEE EETAN MIKROH
5. TOH LEPTOH PSAREE EETAN KAKOH
6. TOH KAKOH CHTAPOTHEE EETAN EESEEHOH
7. EE MIKREE METHOOSA EETAN LEPTEE
8. EE LEPTEE PETALOOTHA EENAH KALEE
9. EE KAKEE HELONA EETAN EESEEHEE

The answers are:

1. THE SMALL FLY IS BAD
2. THE GOOD DOG IS THIN
3. THE BAD HEN WAS QUIET
4. THE GOOD RABBIT WAS SMALL
5. THE THIN FISH WAS BAD
6. THE BAD OCTOPUS WAS QUIET
7. THE SMALL JELLYFISH WAS THIN
8. THE THIN BUTTERFLY IS GOOD
9. THE BAD TORTOISE WAS QUIET

Now cover up the answers below and translate the following:

(You can write your answers in)

1. THE SMALL SALMON IS THIN
2. THE QUIET FISH WAS BAD
3. THE THIN FLY WAS GOOD
4. THE SMALL JELLYFISH WAS BAD
5. THE BAD WASP IS QUIET
6. THE GOOD HORSE WAS SMALL
7. THE THIN RABBIT IS GOOD

The answers are:

1. OH MIKROS SOLOMOS EENAH LEPTOS
2. TOH EESEEHOH PSAREE EETAN KAKOH
3. EE LEPTEE MEEYA EETAN KALEE
4. EE MIKREE METHOOSA EETAN KAKEE
5. EE KAKEE SFEEKA EENAH EESEEHEE
6. TOH KALOH ALORROH EETAN MIKROH
7. TOH LEPTOH KOONELEE EENAH KALOH

IMPORTANT NOTE
Some of the sentences in this course might strike you as being a bit odd!

However, they have been carefully constructed to make you think much more about what you are translating. This helps the memory process and gets away from the idea of learning useful phrases "parrot fashion".

But, of course, having learned with the help of these seemingly odd sentences, you can easily construct your own sentences to suit your particular needs.

Section 2   HOTEL/HOME, FURNITURE, COLOURS

THINK OF EACH IMAGE IN YOUR MIND'S EYE FOR ABOUT TEN SECONDS

○ The Greek for BED is KREVATEE
  Imagine going to bed wearing a CRAVAT.

○ The Greek for TABLE is TRAPEZEE
  Imagine some child using your good table as a TRAPEZE to swing from.

○ The Greek for CHAIR is KAREKLA
  Imagine a CAR WRECKS A chair.

○ The Greek for CURTAIN is COORTEENA
  Imagine you CONCERTINA curtains together.

○ The Greek for PIANO is PIANOH
  Imagine a Greek god playing a piano.

○ The Greek for CLOCK is ROLOEE
  Imagine you always RELY on your clock.

○ The Greek for SHELF is RAFEE
  Imagine you win a shelf in a RAFFLE.

○ The Greek for DRAWER is SIRTAREE
  Imagine an Indian playing a SITAR in a drawer.

○ The Greek for CARPET is HALEE
  Imagine a HOLY carpet.

○ The Greek for ARMCHAIR is POLEETHRONA
  Imagine an armchair is a THRONE for Queen Polly – a POLYTHRONE.

YOU CAN WRITE YOUR ANSWERS IN

○ What is the English for POLEETHRONA? _____

○ What is the English for HALEE? _____

○ What is the English for SIRTAREE? _____

○ What is the English for RAFEE? _____

○ What is the English for ROLOEE? _____

○ What is the English for PIANOH? _____

○ What is the English for COORTEENA? _____

○ What is the English for KAREKLA? _____

○ What is the English for TRAPEZEE? _____

○ What is the English for KREVATEE? _____

TURN BACK FOR THE ANSWERS

COVER UP THE LEFT HAND PAGE BEFORE
ANSWERING

○ What is the Greek for armchair?   _____

○ What is the Greek for carpet?   _____

○ What is the Greek for drawer?   _____

○ What is the Greek for shelf?   _____

○ What is the Greek for clock?   _____

○ What is the Greek for piano?   _____

○ What is the Greek for curtain?   _____

○ What is the Greek for chair?   _____

○ What is the Greek for table?   _____

○ What is the Greek for bed?   _____

TURN BACK FOR THE ANSWERS

SOME MORE DESCRIPTIVE WORDS

THINK OF EACH IMAGE IN YOUR MIND'S EYE FOR ABOUT TEN SECONDS

- The Greek for BEAUTIFUL is OREOH
  Imagine giving a beautiful girl A ROW in a rowing boat.

- The Greek for SWEET is RRLEEKOH
  Imagine you eat a sweet LEEK OH!

- The Greek for YOUNG is NEOH
  Imagine all the young people having to KNEEL before you.

- The Greek for STUPID is HAZOH
  Imagine a stupid HASSLE.

- The Greek for DARK is SKOTEENOH
  Imagine that Scotland has long dark winters, so SCOTTIES KNOW the dark.

*These words have been given with neuter endings. Remember that PR is pronounced very softly at the back of the throat.

YOU CAN WRITE YOUR ANSWERS IN

○ What is the English for SKOTEENOH? _____

○ What is the English for HAZOH? _____

○ What is the English for NEOH? _____

○ What is the English for RRLEEKOH? _____

○ What is the English for OREOH? _____

TURN BACK FOR THE ANSWERS

COVER UP THE LEFT HAND PAGE BEFORE
ANSWERING

○ What is the Greek for dark? _____

○ What is the Greek for stupid? _____

○ What is the Greek for young? _____

○ What is the Greek for sweet? _____

○ What is the Greek for beautiful? _____

TURN BACK FOR THE ANSWERS

N.B. NEOH also means NEW.

SOME SIMPLE VERBS

THINK OF EACH IMAGE IN YOUR MIND'S EYE FOR ABOUT TEN SECONDS

○ The Greek for HAS is ECHEE*
  Imagine he has an EGGY face.

○ The Greek for WANTS is THELEE
  Imagine he wants to be SILLY.

○ The Greek for EATS is TROEE
  Imagine your mother always eats from a TRAY.

○ The Greek for SEES is VLEPEE
  Imagine you see birds FLAPPING about.

* Remember the CH is pronounced like the CH in loch.

YOU CAN WRITE YOUR ANSWERS IN

○ What is the English for VLEPEE? _____

○ What is the English for TROEE? _____

○ What is the English for THELEE? _____

○ What is the English for ECHEE? _____

TURN BACK FOR THE ANSWERS

COVER UP THE LEFT HAND PAGE BEFORE ANSWERING

○ What is the Greek for sees? _____

○ What is the Greek for eats? _____

○ What is the Greek for wants? _____

○ What is the Greek for has? _____

TURN BACK FOR THE ANSWERS

ELEMENTARY GRAMMAR

As was explained in the previous section, in Greek words like thin, young, etc. change their ending according to whether the word they go with is masculine, feminine or neuter.

For example,

> THE THIN DOG (m) is OH LEPTOS SKEELOS
> THE THIN CAT (f) is EE LEPTEE RRATA
> THE THIN BIRD (n) is TOH LEPTOH POOLEE

You have just learned the adjectives beautiful (OREOH), sweet (RRLEEKOH), young (NEOH), stupid (HAZOH) and dark (SKOTEENOH).

So,

> THE BEAUTIFUL DOG   is OH OREOS SKEELOS
> THE BEAUTIFUL CAT   is EE OREA RRATA
> THE BEAUTIFUL FISH is TOH OREOH PSAREE

Please note:

In the above example the feminine ends with -A and not with -EE.

Some feminine adjectives end with -A, but you don't need to worry if you make the occasional mistake and confuse the -A ending with the -EE ending.

You will be understood.

So,

> THE YOUNG SALMON is OH NEOS SOLOMOS
> THE YOUNG CHAIR is EE NEA KAREKLA
> THE YOUNG BED   is TOH NEOH KREVATEE

and:

> THE SWEET DOG   is OH RRLEEKOS SKEELOS
> THE SWEET HEN   is EE RRLEEKYA KOTA
> THE SWEET BIRD is TOH RRLEEKOH POOLEE

Please note that RRLEEKYA is the feminine singular.

Later on you will learn RRLEKA, which is the neuter plural.

But most other adjectives take the feminine ending as usual:

So,

    THE STUPID WASP   is EE HAZEE SFEEKA
    THE DARK JELLYFISH is EE SKOTEENEE
                                  METHOOSA

Now cover up the answers below and translate the following:

(You can write your answer in)

1. EE HAZEE HYEENA TROEE TOH KREVATEE
2. EE RRLEEKYA RRATA VLEPEE TOH HAZOH HALEE
3. TOH OREOH KOONELEE THELEE TOH TRAPEZEE
4. TOH SKOTEENOH ROLOEE VLEPEE TOH RAFEE
5. OH NEOS SKEELOS ECHEE TOH MIKROH SIRTAREE

The answers are:

1. THE STUPID GOOSE EATS THE BED
2. THE SWEET CAT SEES THE STUPID CARPET
3. THE BEAUTIFUL RABBIT WANTS THE TABLE
4. THE DARK CLOCK SEES THE SHELF
5. THE YOUNG DOG HAS THE SMALL DRAWER

Now cover up the answers below and translate the following:

(You can write your answers in)

1. THE YOUNG HORSE WANTS THE BED
2. THE DARK TORTOISE HAS THE TABLE
3. THE BEAUTIFUL ARMCHAIR EATS THE PIANO
4. THE STUPID FISH SEES THE SHELF
5. THE SWEET CURTAIN SEES THE CLOCK

The answers are:

1. TOH NEOH ALORROH THELEE TOH KREVATEE
2. EE SKOTEENEE HELONA ECHEE TOH TRAPEZEE
3. EE OREA POLEETHRONA TROEE TOH PIANOH
4. TOH HAZOH PSAREE VLEPEE TOH RAFEE
5. EE RRLEEKYA COORTEENA VLEPEE TOH ROLOEE

COLOURS

THINK OF EACH IMAGE IN YOUR MIND'S EYE FOR ABOUT TEN SECONDS

○ The Greek for COLOUR is CHROMA (n)
Imagine CHROMATIC colour.

○ The Greek for WHITE is ASPROH
Imagine ASPIRINS are white.

○ The Greek for BLACK is MAVROH
Imagine your MARROW is all black.

○ The Greek for GREY is GREE
Imagine a Greek god, his face all grey and drawn.

○ The Greek for BLUE is BLE
Imagine a Greek god with a blue face.

○ The Greek for GREEN is PRASEENOH
Imagine some BRASS IS NOW covered with a green coating.

○ The Greek for BROWN is KAFE
Imagine sitting in a CAFE all painted brown.

○ The Greek for RED is KOKEENOH
Imagine a red COCONUT.

YOU CAN WRITE YOUR ANSWERS IN

○ What is the English for KOKEENOH? _____

○ What is the English for KAFE? _____

○ What is the English for PRASEENOH? _____

○ What is the English for BLE? _____

○ What is the English for GREE? _____

○ What is the English for MAVROH? _____

○ What is the English for ASPROH? _____

○ What is the English for CHROMA? _____

TURN BACK FOR THE ANSWERS

COVER UP THE LEFT HAND PAGE BEFORE ANSWERING

○ What is the Greek for red? _____

○ What is the Greek for brown? _____

○ What is the Greek for green? _____

○ What is the Greek for blue? _____

○ What is the Greek for grey? _____

○ What is the Greek for black? _____

○ What is the Greek for white? _____

○ What is the Greek for colour? _____

TURN BACK FOR THE ANSWERS

ELEMENTARY GRAMMAR

You have just learned the names for seven colours:

WHITE	ASPROH
BLACK	MAVROH
GREEN	PRASEENOH
RED	KOKEENOH
BROWN	KAFE
BLUE	BLE
GREY	GREE

In sentences such as:

THE DOG IS BLACK you say OH SKEELOS EENAH MAVROS

THE CAT IS WHITE you say EE RRATA EENAH ASPREE

THE TABLE IS RED you say TOH TRAPEZEE EENAH KONEENOH

In other words you use the colour as an adjective.

So, like all adjectives in Greek, the words for colours change their ending according to whether the word they go with is masculine, feminine or neuter.

For example,

TOH KREVATEE EENAH PRASEENOH is THE BED IS GREEN

EE KAREKLA EENAH ASPREE is THE CHAIR IS WHITE

EE PAPYA EENAH KOKEENEE is THE DUCK IS RED

OH SKEELOS EETAN MAVROS is THE DOG WAS BLACK

Now, KAFE (brown), BLE (blue) and GREE (grey) DO NOT change according to the gender of the word they go with.

For example,

THE BROWN CAT is EE KAFE RRATA
THE GREY DUCK is EE GREE PAPYA
THE BLUE CHAIR is EE BLE KAREKLA
THE BLUE SALMON is OH BLE SOLOMOS

Imagine brown cows, grey geese and blue bottles NEVER change their colours.

You need not worry if you confuse these endings and you make occasional mistakes. You will still be understood.

Now cover up the answers below and translate the following:

(You can write your answers in)

1. EE MIKREE PAPYA EENAH KOKEENEE
2. OH KAKOS SKEELOS EENAH KAFE
3. TOH MAVROH ENDOMOH EENAH KALOH
4. EE ASPREE RRATA EENAH LEPTEE
5. TOH PRASEENOH TRAPEZEE EETAN MIKROH

The answers are:

1. THE SMALL DUCK IS RED
2. THE BAD DOG IS BROWN
3. THE BLACK INSECT IS GOOD
4. THE WHITE CAT IS THIN
5. THE GREEN TABLE WAS SMALL

Now cover up the answers below and translate the following:

(You can write your answers in)

1. THE GREY DUCK IS SMALL
2. THE BLUE DOG IS YOUNG
3. THE GREEN CHAIR IS BAD
4. THE RED CLOCK IS THIN
5. THE WHITE SALMON WAS QUIET

The answers are:

1. EE GREE PAPYA EENAH MIKREE
2. OH BLE SKEELOS EENAH NEOS
3. EE PRASEENEE KAREKLA EENAH KAKEE
4. TOH KOKEENOH ROLOEE EENAH LEPTOH
5. OH ASPROS SOLOMOS EETAN EESEEHOS

PARTS OF A HOUSE

THINK OF EACH IMAGE IN YOUR MIND'S EYE FOR ABOUT TEN SECONDS

○ The Greek for STAIRCASE is SKALA
Imagine the staircase at LA SCALA Milan, the famous opera house.

○ The Greek for FLOOR is PATOMA (n)
Imagine you should always PAT ON A floor in a house before you live in it.

○ The Greek for KITCHEN is KOOZEENA
Imagine being COSY IN A kitchen.

N.B. KOOZEENA also means COOKER.

○ The Greek for ROOM is KAMARA
Imagine entering a room filled with CAMERAS.

○ The Greek for BEDROOM is KREVATOH-KAMARA
Imagine cravats all over your bedroom – KREVATOH KAMERA.

○ The Greek for WALL is TEECHOS
Imagine you can't have your TEA 'CAUSE the wall just fell down.

○ The Greek for DOOR is PORTA
Imagine asking a PORTER to open your door.

○ The Greek for GARDEN is KEEPOS
Imagine our parents used to KEEP US kids in the garden.

○ The Greek for CLOAKROOM is GUARDAROBA
Imagine you tell someone to GUARD A ROBE in the cloakroom.

○ The Greek for DINING ROOM is TRAPEZAREEA
Imagine your dining room is a TRAPEZE AREA.

YOU CAN WRITE YOUR ANSWERS IN

○ What is the English for TRAPEZAREEA? _____

○ What is the English for GUARDAROBA? _____

○ What is the English for KEEPOS? _____

○ What is the English for PORTA? _____

○ What is the English for TEECHOS? _____

○ What is the English for
  KREVATOH-KAMARA? _____

○ What is the English for KAMARA? _____

○ What is the English for KOOZEENA? _____

○ What is the English for PATOMA (n)? _____

○ What is the English for SKALA? _____

TURN BACK FOR THE ANSWERS

COVER UP THE LEFT HAND PAGE BEFORE ANSWERING

○ What is the Greek for dining room? _____

○ What is the Greek for cloakroom? _____

○ What is the Greek for garden? _____

○ What is the Greek for door? _____

○ What is the Greek for wall? _____

○ What is the Greek for bedroom? _____

○ What is the Greek for room? _____

○ What is the Greek for kitchen? _____

○ What is the Greek for floor? _____

○ What is the Greek for staircase? _____

TURN BACK FOR THE ANSWERS

Note: Another word for room is dhomatio

SOME USEFUL CONNECTING WORDS

THINK OF EACH IMAGE IN YOUR MIND'S EYE FOR ABOUT TEN SECONDS

○ The Greek for AND is KEE
Imagine doors have locks AND KEYS.

N.B. KEE (and) is KEE in front of a vowel and KEH in front of a consonant.

○ The Greek for BUT is ALAH
Imagine saying, "BUT for ALLAH I would be nothing."

○ The Greek for OR is EE
Imagine thinking "HE OR she".

○ The Greek for NOT is THEN
Imagine I never tied a knot, not THEN, not ever.

YOU CAN WRITE YOUR ANSWERS IN

○ What is the English for THEN   _____

○ What is the English for EE?   _____

○ What is the English for ALAH?   _____

○ What is the English for KEE?   _____

TURN BACK FOR THE ANSWERS

COVER UP THE LEFT HAND PAGE BEFORE
ANSWERING

○ What is the Greek for not? _____

○ What is the Greek for or? _____

○ What is the Greek for but? _____

○ What is the Greek for and? _____

TURN BACK FOR THE ANSWERS

ELEMENTARY GRAMMAR

As you have just learnt, in Greek, the word for NOT is THEN.

So,

THE DOG DOES NOT SEE	is OH SKEELOS THEN VLEPEE
THE CAT DOES NOT HAVE	is EE RRATA THEN ECHEE
THE BIRD DOES NOT EAT	is TOH POOLEE THEN TROEE
THE HORSE DOES NOT WANT	is TOH ALORROH THEN THELEE

Now cover up the answers below and translate the following:

(You can write your answers in)

1. EE RRLEEKYA RRATA ECHEE TOH FEETHEE KEH THEN ECHEE TOH TRAPEZEE

2. OH SKOTEENOS SKEELOS THELEE TOH RAFEE EE TOH ROLOEE

3. EE ASPREE HYEENA VLEPEE TOH TRAPEZEE EE TOH PATOMA

4. EE KOKEENEE MEEYA VLEPEE TOH HALEE ALAH THEN VLEPEE TOH SIRTAREE

5. TOH GREE KOONOOPEE TROEE TOH RRLEEKOH PSAREE KEH TOH KAFE POOLEE

The answers are:

1. THE SWEET CAT HAS THE SNAKE AND DOES NOT HAVE THE TABLE

2. THE DARK DOG WANTS THE SHELF OR THE CLOCK

3. THE WHITE GOOSE SEES THE TABLE OR THE FLOOR

4. THE RED FLY SEES THE CARPET BUT DOES NOT SEE THE DRAWER

5. THE GREY MOSQUITO EATS THE SWEET FISH AND THE BROWN BIRD

Now cover up the answers below and translate the following:

(You can write your answers in)

1. THE BROWN SALMON SEES THE BED AND DOES NOT SEE THE FLOOR

2. THE GREEN DOG HAS THE SHELF AND DOES NOT HAVE THE TABLE

3. THE RED TORTOISE WANTS THE CLOCK AND DOES NOT WANT THE CARPET

4. THE SALMON HAS THE GREEN FLOOR OR THE BLUE BIRD

5. THE BLACK DUCK EATS THE SWEET FISH OR THE YOUNG INSECT

The answers are:

1. OH KAFE SOLOMOS VLEPEE TOH KREVATEE KEH THEN VLEPEE TOH PATOMA

2. OH PRASEENOS SKEELOS ECHEE TOH RAFEE KEH THEN ECHEE TOH TRAPEZEE

3. EE KOKEENEE HELONA THELEE TOH ROLOEE KEH THEN THELEE TOH HALEE

4. OH SOLOMOS ECHEE TOH PRASEENO PATOMA EE TOH BLE POOLEE

5. EE MAVREE PAPYA TROEE TOH RRLEEKO PSAREE EE TOH NEOH ENDOMOH

70

Section 3 CLOTHES/FAMILY WORDS

THINK OF EACH IMAGE IN YOUR MIND'S EYE FOR ABOUT TEN SECONDS

○ HAT is KAPELOH
Imagine a CAP on your head instead of a hat.

○ SHOE is PAPOOTSEE
Imagine your PA PUTS HIS shoe on your foot.

○ TROUSERS is PANTELONEE
Imagine wearing baggy PANTELOONS instead of trousers.

○ SKIRT is FOOSTA
Imagine being told to get your skirt on FASTER next time.

○ BLOUSE is BLOOSA
Imagine a BLUE blouse.

○ COAT is PALTOH
Imagine getting a PAL TO lend you his coat.

○ BATHING SUIT is MAHYOH
Imagine thinking, "MAY YOU not be seen dead in a bathing suit."

○ DRESS is FOOSTANEE
Imagine when you put a dress on, FIRST A KNEE then an ankle appears.

○ JACKET is ZAKETA
Imagine a Greek god wearing a dinner jacket.

○ JUMPER (or PULLOVER) is POOLOVER
Imagine a Greek god putting a pullover on.

YOU CAN WRITE YOUR ANSWERS IN

○ What is the English for POOLOVER? _____

○ What is the English for ZAKETA? _____

○ What is the English for FOOSTANEE? _____

○ What is the English for MAYOH? _____

○ What is the English for PALTOH? _____

○ What is the English for BLOOSA? _____

○ What is the English for FOOSTA? _____

○ What is the English for PANTELONEE? _____

○ What is the English for PAPOOTSEE? _____

○ What is the English for KAPELOH? _____

TURN BACK FOR THE ANSWERS

72

COVER UP THE LEFT HAND PAGE BEFORE
ANSWERING

○ What is the Greek for jumper or pullover? _____

○ What is the Greek for jacket? _____

○ What is the Greek for dress? _____

○ What is the Greek for bathing suit? _____

○ What is the Greek for coat? _____

○ What is the Greek for blouse? _____

○ What is the Greek for skirt? _____

○ What is the Greek for trousers? _____

○ What is the Greek for shoe? _____

○ What is the Greek for hat? _____

TURN BACK FOR THE ANSWERS

Notes
1. Another word for DRESS is FOREMA.
2. The word ZAKETA normally refers to a female's clothing. A male wears
   a SAKAKI or SAKOS.

73

THE FAMILY

**THINK OF EACH IMAGE IN YOUR MIND'S EYE FOR ABOUT
TEN SECONDS**

○ The Greek for FATHER is PATERAS (m)
Imagine you hear feet PATTER AS your father comes to say
"Goodnight".

○ The Greek for MOTHER is MEETERA
Imagine your mother getting drunk on MADEIRA wine.

○ The Greek for BROTHER is ATHELFOS
Imagine you should always give into brothers OR THEY'LL
FUSS.

○ The Greek for SISTER is ATHELFEE
Imagine I SELL FEET to your sister.

○ The Greek for SON is YOS
Imagine saying, "YES, I have a son."

○ The Greek for DAUGHTER is KOREE
Imagine you CARRY your daughter everywhere.

○ The Greek for HUSBAND is ANDRAS (m)
Imagine your husband has to UNDRESS every night.
N.B. ANDRAS also means MAN.

○ The Greek for WIFE is YEENEKA
Imagine YOU NECK A wife – every day.
N.B. YEENEKA also means WOMAN.

○ The Greek for BOY is ARROHREE
Imagine I HURRY when I see a boy.

○ The Greek for GIRL is KOREETSEE
Imagine a girl is always CORRECT, SEE!

YOU CAN WRITE YOUR ANSWERS IN

○ What is the English for KOREETSEE? _____

○ What is the English for ARROHREE? _____

○ What is the English for YEENEKA? _____

○ What is the English for ANDRAS (m)? _____

○ What is the English for KOREE? _____

○ What is the English for YOS? _____

○ What is the English for ATHELFEE? _____

○ What is the English for ATHELFOS? _____

○ What is the English for MEETERA? _____

○ What is the English for PATERAS (m)? _____

TURN BACK FOR THE ANSWERS

COVER UP THE LEFT HAND PAGE BEFORE ANSWERING

○ What is the Greek for girl? _____

○ What is the Greek for boy? _____

○ What is the Greek for wife? _____

○ What is the Greek for husband? _____

○ What is the Greek for daughter? _____

○ What is the Greek for son? _____

○ What is the Greek for sister? _____

○ What is the Greek for brother? _____

○ What is the Greek for mother? _____

○ What is the Greek for father? _____

TURN BACK FOR THE ANSWERS

ELEMENTARY GRAMMAR

QUESTIONS

In Greek it is very easy to ask questions, because all you have to do is to change the tone of your voice accordingly.

So,

    to say IS THE DOG THIN?

    you simply say OH SKEELOS EENAH LEPTOS?

    (The dog is thin?)

IS THE CAT BEAUTIFUL?	is EE RRATA EENAH OREA?
DOES THE CAT HAVE THE INSECT?	is EE RRATA ECHEE TOH ENDOMOH?
DOES THE GIRL SEE THE BIRD?	is TOH KOREETSEE VLEPEE TOH POOLEE?

The same happens when you ask in the negative.

For example,

ISN'T THE BLOUSE SMALL?	is EE BLOOSA THEN EENAH MIKREE?
(the blouse not is small?)	
DOESN'T THE FATHER HAVE THE COAT?	is OH PATERAS THEN ECHEE TOH PALTOH?
(the father not has the coat?)	

78

Now cover up the answers below and translate the following:

(You can write your answers in)

1. EE MEETERA EENAH NEA?
2. OH PATERAS THEN THELEE TOH PANTELONEE?
3. TOH KOREETSEE THEN TROEE TOH KOONELEE?
4. EE ATHELFEE THEN VLEPEE TOH TRAPEZEE?
5. OH YOS THEN EENAH RRLEEKOS?

The answers are:

1. IS THE MOTHER YOUNG?
2. DOESN'T THE FATHER WANT THE TROUSERS?
3. DOESN'T THE GIRL EAT THE RABBIT?
4. DOESN'T THE SISTER SEE THE TABLE?
5. ISN'T THE SON SWEET?

Note: in Greek the question mark is ; (like the English semi-colon).

Now cover up the answer below and translate the following:

(You can write your answers in)

1. IS THE ROOM SMALL?
2. DOES THE MOTHER WANT THE HAT?
3. ISN'T THE SKIRT BEAUTIFUL?
4. DOES THE BROTHER EAT THE FISH?
5. DOESN'T THE BOY SEE THE BED?

The answers are:

1. EE KAMARA EENAH MIKREE?
2. EE MEETERA THELEE TOH KAPELOH?
3. EE FOOSTA THEN EENAH OREA?
4. OH ATHELFOS TROEE TOH PSAREE?
5. TOH ARROHREE THEN VLEPEE TOH KREVATEE?

SOME USEFUL WORDS

THINK OF EACH IMAGE IN YOUR MIND'S EYE FOR ABOUT TEN SECONDS

○ The Greek for ONLY is MONOH
Imagine thinking that a MONOcle is only one glass.

○ The Greek for VERY is POLEE
Imagine thinking, "That is very POLITE."

○ The Greek for YES is NEH
Imagine being told, "NEver say yes."

○ The Greek for NO is OCHEE
Imagine a Scotsman saying, "OCH, HE'S no stupid!"

○ The Greek for ALSO is EPEESEES
Imagine A PIECE IS also part of the whole.

YOU CAN WRITE YOUR ANSWERS IN

○ What is the English for EPEESEES? _____

○ What is the English for OCHEE? _____

○ What is the English for NEH? _____

○ What is the English for POLEE? _____

○ What is the English for MONOH? _____

TURN BACK FOR THE ANSWERS

COVER UP THE LEFT HAND PAGE BEFORE ANSWERING

○ What is the Greek for also? _____

○ What is the Greek for no? _____

○ What is the Greek for yes? _____

○ What is the Greek for very? _____

○ What is the Greek for only? _____

TURN BACK FOR THE ANSWERS

ELEMENTARY GRAMMAR

In sentences such as THE DOG SEES THE CAT, the cat is the object of the sentence.

In other words, the cat is having something done to it.

So, in the sentences:

> THE GIRL SEES THE BATHING SUIT
> (TOH KOREETSEE VLEPPE TOH MAHYOH)
>
> THE GIRL WANTS THE BATHING SUITE
> (TOH KOREETSEE THELEE TOH MAHYOH)
>
> THE DOG EATS THE BATHING SUIT
> (OH SKEELOS TROEE TOH MAHYOH)

the bathing suit (TOH MAHYOH) is the object of the sentence.

In Greek, when the object of the sentence is FEMININE, then the word for THE becomes TEEN.

Imagine TEENagers are girls.

So, to say   THE DOG WANTS THE CAT
you say   OH SKEELOS THELEE TEEN RRATA

> THE BOY SEES THE SISTER is TOH ARROHREE
>   VLEPEE TEEN
>   ATHELFEE

Please note that the neuter word does not change when it is the object of the sentence.

For example,

> THE CAT HAS THE HAT is EE RRATA ECHEE TOH
>   KAPELOH

Now cover up the answers below and translate the following:

(You can write your answers in)

1. EE ATHELFEE ECHEE TEEN KAREKLA, ALAH OH YOS
   THEN ECHEE TOH PANTELONEE

2. NEH, EE MEETERA VLEPEE TEEN SKALA KEE OH
   PATERAS VLEPEE TEEN ATHELFEE

3. OCHEE, OH YOS TROEE PSAREE ALAH EE KOREE
   THEN TROEE TEEN METHOOSA

4. EE KOREE THELEE TEEN FOOSTA ALAH THEN
   THELEE TEEN BLE BLOOSA

5. OH SKEELOS TROEE TEEN METHOOSA KEH MONOH
   EE RRATA TROEE TOH PAPOOTSEE

The answers are:

1. THE SISTER HAS THE CHAIR, BUT THE SON DOESN'T
   HAVE THE TROUSERS

2. YES, THE MOTHER SEES THE STAIRCASE AND THE
   FATHER SEES THE SISTER

3. NO, THE SON EATS FISH BUT THE DAUGHTER
   DOESN'T EAT THE JELLYFISH

4. THE DAUGHTER WANTS THE SKIRT BUT DOESN'T
   WANT THE BLUE BLOUSE

5. THE DOG EATS THE JELLYFISH AND ONLY THE CAT
   EATS THE SHOE

Now cover up the answers below and translate the following:

(You can write your answers in)

1. THE GIRL WANTS THE SKIRT, BUT THE BOY ONLY WANTS THE CAT

2. THE FATHER SEES THE CHAIR, OR THE JACKET

3. NO, THE BOY EATS THE DUCK AND SEES THE VERY BLACK BIRD

4. YES, THE MAN WANTS THE WOMAN, AND ALSO THE BUTTERFLY

5. THE DOG HAS THE BIRD, BUT THE CAT HAS THE GREEN HAT

The answers are:

1. TOH KOREETSEE THELEE TEEN FOOSTA, ALAH TOH ARROHREE THELEE MONOH TEEN RRATA

2. OH PATERAS VLEPEE TEEN KAREKLA EE TEEN ZAKETA

3. OCHEE, TOH ARROHREE TROEE TEEN PAPYA KEH VLEPEE TOH POLEE MAVROH POOLEE

4. NEH, OH ANDRAS THELEE TEEN YEENEKA, KEE EPEESEES TEEN PETALOOTHA

5. OH SKEELOS ECHEE TOH POOLEE, ALAH EE RRATA ECHEE TOH PRASEENOH KAPELOH

SOME MORE USEFUL WORDS

THINK OF EACH IMAGE IN YOUR MIND'S EYE FOR ABOUT TEN SECONDS

○ MALE FRIEND is FEELOS
Imagine telling your male friend you FEEL LOSt without him.

○ FEMALE FRIEND is FEELEE
Imagine your female friend has a lively FILLY.

○ MORNING is PROYEE
Imagine you PRAY for morning to come.

○ NIGHT is NICHTA
Imagine someone NICKED a jewel at night.

○ RAIN is VROCHEE (f)
Imagine rain like ROCKETS pounding on a roof.

○ NUMBER is ARITHMOS
Imagine you use numbers for ARITHMETIC.

○ NAME is ONOMA (n)
Imagine saying to someone, "HONOUR MY name".

○ PAPER is HARTEE
Imagine the prisoner ate a HEARTY meal of paper before his execution.

○ PEN is STEELOH
Imagine a STEEL pen.

○ BATH is BANYOH
Imagine they BAN YOU from using your own bath.
N.B. BANYOH is also the word for bathroom.

YOU CAN WRITE YOU ANSWERS IN

○ What is the English for BANYOH? _____

○ What is the English for STEELOH? _____

○ What is the English for HARTEE? _____

○ What is the English for ONOMA (n)? _____

○ What is the English for ARITHMOS? _____

○ What is the English for VROCHEE (f)? _____

○ What is the English for NICHTA? _____

○ What is the English for PROYEE? _____

○ What is the English for FEELEE? _____

○ What is the English for FEELOS? _____

TURN BACK FOR THE ANSWERS

COVER UP THE LEFT HAND PAGE BEFORE ANSWERING

○ What is the Greek for bath? _____

○ What is the Greek for pen? _____

○ What is the Greek for paper? _____

○ What is the Greek for name? _____

○ What is the Greek for number? _____

○ What is the Greek for rain? _____

○ What is the Greek for night? _____

○ What is the Greek for morning? _____

○ What is the Greek for female friend? _____

○ What is the Greek for male friend? _____

TURN BACK FOR THE ANSWERS

N.B. Another word for PEN is PENAH.

ELEMENTARY GRAMMAR

You have just seen that when the object of the sentence is a feminine word like THE CAT (EE RRATA), the word for THE becomes TEEN.

For example,

OH SKEELOS TROEE TEEN RRATA is THE DOG EATS THE CAT

For MASCULINE words, the word for THE becomes TON.

Imagine a TON weight on a boy.

The masculine word itself also changes, when it is the object of the sentence, from SKEELOS to SKEELO.

In other words, you drop the -S ending.

So,

THE FATHER SEES THE SALMON	is OH PATERAS VLEPEE TON SOLOMO
THE DOG EATS THE LOBSTER	is OH SKEELOS TROEE TON ASTAKO
THE SISTER HAS THE DOG	is EE ATHELFEE ECHEE TON SKEELO

Now cover up the answers below and translate the following:

(You can write your answers in)

1. TOH ALORROH VLEPEE TON KEEPO KEH TOH ONOMA

2. EE SFEEKA VLEPEE TON TEECHO KEH TON ARITHMO

3. EE MELEESA TROEE TON SKEELO KEH TOH STEELOH

4. EE ATHELFEE THELEE TON ATHELFO KEH TOH PRO-
   YEE KEE TEEN NICHTA

5. EE MEETERA ECHEE TON YO KEH TEEN FEELEE

The answers are:

1. THE HORSE SEES THE GARDEN AND THE NAME

2. THE WASP SEES THE WALL AND THE NUMBER

3. THE BEE EATS THE DOG AND THE PEN

4. THE SISTER WANTS THE BROTHER AND THE MORN-
   ING AND THE NIGHT

5. THE MOTHER HAS THE SON AND THE FEMALE
   FRIEND

Now cover up the answers below and translate the following:

(You can write your answers in)

1. THE MOTHER SEES THE GARDEN AND THE MALE FRIEND

2. THE HEN SEES THE WALL BUT DOES NOT SEE THE RAIN

3. YES, THE GIRL HAS THE DOG AND THE DOG HAS THE PAPER

4. THE DOG EATS THE BROTHER OR THE PEN

5. THE SISTER WANTS THE SALMON AND THE SALMON WANTS THE BATH

The answers are:

1. EE MEETERA VLEPEE TON KEEPO KEH TON FEELO

2. EE KOTA VLEPEE TON TEECHO ALAH THEN VLEPEE TEEN VROCHEE

3. NEH, TOH KOREETSEE ECHEE TON SKEELO KEE OH SKEELOS ECHEE TOH HARTEE

4. OH SKEELOS TROEE TON ATHELFO EE TOH STEELOH

5. EE ATHELFEE THELEE TON SOLOMO KEE OH SOLOMOS THELEE TOH BANYOH

Section 4 IN THE COUNTRY, TIME WORDS

THINK OF EACH IMAGE IN YOUR MIND'S EYE FOR ABOUT TEN SECONDS

○ The Greek for TREE is THENDROH
Imagine a tree is in the CENTRE O' a field.

○ The Greek for PLANT is FEETOH
Imagine putting your FEET ON a valuable plant.

○ The Greek for FRUIT is FROOTOH
Imagine a Greek god eating fruit.

○ The Greek for EARTH is CHOMA (n)*
Imagine every time you eat earth, you will end up in a COMA.

○ The Greek for CARROT is CAROTOH
Imagine Greek gods sprouting carrots from their hair.

○ The Greek for ONION is KREMEETHEE
Imagine onions CREAM EASY.

○ The Greek for Apple is MEELOH
Imagine a MEAL O' apples.

○ The Greek for MELON is PEPONEE
Imagine you only BUY BONNY melons in Scotland.

○ The Greek for GRAPES is STAFEELYA
Imagine you need grapeS TO FILL YOU.

○ The Greek for FIGS is SEEKA
Imagine you SEEK A fig everywhere.

*Remember the CH is pronounced like the CH in LOCH.

YOU CAN WRITE YOUR ANSWERS IN

○ What is the English for SEEKA? _____

○ What is the English for STAFEELYA? _____

○ What is the English for PEPONEE? _____

○ What is the English for MEELOH? _____

○ What is the English for KREMEETHEE? _____

○ What is the English for CAROTOH? _____

○ What is the English for CHOMA (n)? _____

○ What is the English for FROOTOH? _____

○ What is the English for FEETOH? _____

○ What is the English for THENDROH? _____

TURN BACK FOR THE ANSWERS

94

○ What is the Greek for figs? _____

○ What is the Greek for grapes? _____

○ What is the Greek for melon? _____

○ What is the Greek for apple? _____

○ What is the Greek for onion? _____

○ What is the Greek for carrot? _____

○ What is the Greek for earth? _____

○ What is the Greek for fruit? _____

○ What is the Greek for plant? _____

○ What is the Greek for tree? _____

TURN BACK FOR THE ANSWERS

TWO USEFUL WORDS

THINK OF EACH IMAGE IN YOUR MIND'S EYE FOR ABOUT TEN SECONDS

○ The Greek for HERE is ETHOH
  Imagine HE SAW me HERE.

○ The Greek for THERE is EKEE
  Imagine you should put A KEY there.

YOU CAN WRITE YOUR ANSWERS IN

○ What is the English for EKEE?　　　_____

○ What is the English for ETHOH?　　_____

TURN BACK FOR THE ANSWERS

COVER UP THE LEFT HAND PAGE BEFORE ANSWERING

○ What is the Greek for there?   ·_____

○ What is the Greek for here?   _____

TURN BACK FOR THE ANSWERS

ELEMENTARY GRAMMAR

The word for I AM, in Greek, is EEMEH.

Imagine I AM a HE MAn.

So, to say I AM THIN you say:

EEMEH LEPTOS if you are male,

and

EEMEH LEPTEE if you are female.

The adjective ending will change according to whether the person talking is a male or a female.

The word for YOU ARE is EESSEH

Imagine YOU ARE EASY to please.

So, to say YOU ARE BEAUTIFUL you say:

EESSEH OREOS if talking to a male, or
EESSEH OREA if you are talking to a female.

The word for HE, SHE or IT IS is EENAH.

Imagine HE, SHE or IT IS IN A house.

So,

HE IS GOOD   is EENAH KALOS
SHE IS QUIET is EENAH EESEEHEE
IT IS BAD   is EENAH KAKOH

Of course, to say I AM NOT you put the THEN before EEMEH.

So,

I AM NOT THIN (for a male)   is THEN EEMEH LEPTOS
YOU ARE NOT YOUNG (for a male) is THEN EESSEH NEOS
SHE IS NOT BAD   is THEN EENAH KAKEE

Now cover up the answers below and translate the following:
(You can write your answers in)

1. EEMEH MIKROS ALAH THEN EEMEH ASPROS EE HAZOS

2. EENAH KAKEE ALAH TOH PEPONEE EENAH MIKROH KEH TOH MEELOH EENAH KOKEENOH

3. EESSEH NEOS KEE EPEESEES EESSEH POLEE OREOS

4. EENAH SKOTEENOH KEE EE NICHTA EENAH MAVREE

5. EEMEH OREA KEH TOH FROOTOH EENAH RRLEEKOH

6. EESSEH LEPTEE ALAH TOH THENDROH EENAH MONOH PRASEENOH

The answers are:

1. I AM SMALL (male) BUT I AM NOT WHITE OR STUPID

2. SHE IS BAD BUT THE MELON IS SMALL AND THE APPLE IS RED

3. YOU ARE YOUNG (male) AND YOU ARE ALSO VERY BEAUTIFUL

4. IT IS DARK AND THE NIGHT IS BLACK

5. I AM BEAUTIFUL (female) AND THE FRUIT IS SWEET

6. YOU ARE THIN (female) BUT THE TREE IS ONLY GREEN

Now cover up the answers below and translate the following:

(You can write your answers in)

1. I AM YOUNG (male)

2. I AM YOUNG (female)

3. YOU ARE STUPID (male)

4. YOU ARE STUPID (female)

5. YOU ARE HERE, BUT THE BEAUTIFUL TREE IS THERE

6. I AM ALSO THERE BUT THE PLANT AND THE FRUIT ARE HERE

7. SHE IS SWEET, BUT THE BROWN EARTH IS QUIET

8. HE IS GOOD, BUT THE RED CARROT IS BAD AND THE GREEN ONION IS BAD

9. IS IT BAD OR IS IT VERY GOOD?

The answers are:

1. EEMEH NEOS

2. EEMEH NEA

3. EESSEH HAZOS

4. EESSEH HAZEE

5. EESSEH ETHOH, ALAH TOH OREOH THENDROH EENAH EKEE

6. EEMEH EPEESEES EKEE ALAH TOH FEETOH KEH TOH FROOTOH EENAH ETHOH

7. EENAH RRLEEKYA, ALAH TOH KAFE CHOMA EENAH EESEEHOH

8. EENAH KALOS ALAH TOH KOKEENOH CAROTOH EENAH KAKOH KEH TOH PRASEENOH KREMEETHEE EENAH KAKOH

9. EENAH KAKOH EE EENAH POLEE KALOH?

TIME

THINK OF EACH IMAGE IN YOUR MIND'S EYE FOR ABOUT TEN SECONDS

○ The Greek for MINUTE is LEPTOH
   Imagine you LEAPT TO your feet once a minute.
   (It is the same word as for THIN)

○ The Greek for HOUR is ORA
   Imagine you wait in HORROR for the hour to strike.

○ The Greek for DAY is MERA
   Imagine a MERRY day with laughing and singing all day.

○ The Greek for WEEK is EVTHOMATHA
   Imagine asking IF THE MOTHER can come for a week.

○ The Greek for MONTH is MEENAS (m)
   Imagine your boss is MEAN AS can be at the end of the
   month.

○ The Greek for YEAR is CHRONOS*
   Imagine they CROWN US once a year.

○ The Greek for TODAY is SEEMERA
   Imagine it is SIMMERing hot today.

○ The Greek for YESTERDAY is CHTHES*
   Imagine IT IS yesterday.

○ The Greek for MIDDAY IS MESSEEMEREE
   Imagine meeting an untidy girlfriend – MESSY MARY – at
   midday.

○ The Greek for MIDNIGHT is MESSANICHTA
   Imagine there is a MESS A NIGHT every midnight.

*Remember CH is pronounced as in LOCH.

YOU CAN WRITE YOUR ANSWERS IN

○ What is the English for MESSANICHTA? _____

○ What is the English for
MESSEEMEREE? _____

○ What is the English for CHTHES? _____

○ What is the English for SEEMERA? _____

○ What is the English for CHRONOS? _____

○ What is the English for MEENAS (m)? _____

○ What is the English for EVTHOMATHA? _____

○ What is the English for MERA? _____

○ What is the English for ORA? _____

○ What is the English for LEPTOH? _____

TURN BACK FOR THE ANSWERS

COVER UP THE LEFT HAND PAGE BEFORE ANSWERING

○ What is the Greek for midnight? _____

○ What is the Greek for midday? _____

○ What is the Greek for yesterday? _____

○ What is the Greek for today? _____

○ What is the Greek for year? _____

○ What is the Greek for month? _____

○ What is the Greek for week? _____

○ What is the Greek for day? _____

○ What is the Greek for hour? _____

○ What is the Greek for minute? _____

TURN BACK FOR THE ANSWERS

SOME MORE USEFUL WORDS

THINK OF EACH IMAGE IN YOUR MIND'S EYE FOR ABOUT TEN SECONDS

○ The Greek for IMMEDIATELY is AMESSOS
Imagine asking someone to give you A MESSAGE immediately.

○ The Greek for MUCH is POLEE
Imagine I like the POLIce very much.

(N.B. MUCH and VERY are the same word)

○ The Greek for MORE is PEEOH POLEE
Imagine there is a campaign for more PIER POLIce to patrol piers.

○ The Greek for ALWAYS is PANDA
Imagine there will always be a PANDA in China.

○ The Greek for NEVER is POTEH
Imagine you should never drive anyone POTTY.

YOU CAN WRITE YOUR ANSWERS IN

○ What is the English for POTEH? _____

○ What is the English for PANDA? _____

○ What is the English for PEEOH POLEE? _____

○ What is the English for POLEE? _____

○ What is the English for AMESSOS? _____

TURN BACK FOR THE ANSWERS

COVER UP THE LEFT HAND PAGE BEFORE
ANSWERING

○ What is the Greek for never? _____

○ What is the Greek for always? _____

○ What is the Greek for more? _____

○ What is the Greek for much? _____

○ What is the Greek for immediately? _____

TURN BACK FOR THE ANSWERS

ELEMENTARY GRAMMAR

To say WE ARE in Greek, you say EEMASTEH.

Imagine saying, "We are HERE MASTER."

To say YOU ARE, when talking to more than one person, you say EESTEH.

Imagine the Pope telling the crowd at St. Peter's Square, "You are welcome for EASTER."

To say THEY ARE you say EENAH.

So,

THEY ARE THERE is EENAH EKEE

THE DOG AND THE CAT ARE THERE is OH SKEELOS KEE EE RRATA EENAH EKEE.

Again, to say WE ARE NOT, you put the THEN before EEMASTEH.

So,

WE ARE NOT HERE is THEN EEMASTEH ETHOH

YOU ARE NEVER HERE is THEN EESTEH POTEH ETHOH

THEY ARE NOT THERE is THEN EENAH EKEE

In Greek, when you want to say WE ARE NEVER HERE, you say, "THEN eemasteh POTEH ethoh."

Similarly, when you want to say HE NEVER SEES THE BIRD, you say, "THEN vlepee POTEH toh poolee."

In other words, you use the negative form of the verb, followed by the word "never".

This is opposite to the use in English.

Now cover up the answers below and translate the following:

(You can write your answers in)

1. THEN EEMASTEH EKEE ALAH EE ORA KEE TOH LEPTOH EENAH ETHOH

2. EESTEH PANDA ETHOH EE EKEE

3. EENAH ETHOH KEE EE EVTHOMATHA KEE OH MEENAS EENAH ETHOH

4. EESTEH EKEE KEE EE MERA EENAH MAVREE

5. THEN EESTEH EKEE ALAH OH MEENAS KEE OH CHRONOS EENAH PANDA ETHOH

6. OH SKEELOS KEE EE RRATA EENAH ETHOH SEEMERA, ALAH OH SKEELOS THEN EETAN EKEE CHTHES

The answers are:

1. WE ARE NOT THERE BUT THE HOUR AND THE MINUTE ARE HERE

2. YOU (plural) ARE ALWAYS HERE OR THERE

3. THEY ARE HERE AND THE WEEK AND THE MONTH ARE HERE

4. YOU (plural) ARE THERE AND THE DAY IS BLACK

5. YOU (plural) ARE NOT THERE BUT THE MONTH AND THE YEAR ARE ALWAYS HERE

6. THE DOG AND THE CAT ARE HERE TODAY, BUT THE DOG WAS NOT THERE YESTERDAY

Now cover up the answers below and translate the following:

(You can write your answers in)

1. YOU (plural) ARE HERE
2. WE ARE THERE MUCH MORE
3. THEY ARE THERE
4. WE ARE NEVER THERE IMMEDIATELY
5. THEY ARE NOT HERE

The answers are:

1. EESTEH ETHOH
2. EEMASTEH EKEE PEEOH POLEE
3. EENAH EKEE
4. THEN EEMASTEH POTEH EKEE AMESSOS
5. THEN EENAH ETHOH

PLEASE NOTE, that EENAH EKEE could also mean HE, SHE or IT IS THERE.

DAYS OF THE WEEK

THINK OF EACH IMAGE IN YOUR MIND'S EYE FOR ABOUT TEN SECONDS

○ The Greek for MONDAY is THEFTERA (f)
Imagine there is a THEFT TERROR every Monday.

○ The Greek for TUESDAY is TREETEE (f)
Imagine a peace TREATY is always signed on a Tuesday.

○ The Greek for WEDNESDAY is TETARTEE (f)
Imagine your girlfriend always looks TOO TARTY on Wednesday.

○ The Greek for THURSDAY is PEMTEE (f)
Imagine you always feel EMPTY on Thursday without peas – PEA EMPTY.

○ The Greek for FRIDAY is PARASKEVEE (f)
Imagine PARA'S SKIVVY on Friday.

○ Imagine The Greek for SATURDAY is SAVATOH (n)
Imagine you SAVE A TOE for Saturday dinner.

○ The Greek for SUNDAY is KEERYAKEE (f)
Imagine I CARRY A KEY on Sundays.

YOU CAN WRITE YOUR ANSWERS IN

○ What is the English for KEERYAKEE (f)? _____

○ What is the English for SAVATOH? _____

○ What is the English for PARASKEVEE (f)? _____

○ What is the English for PEMTEE (f)? _____

○ What is the English for TETARTEE (f)? _____

○ What is the English for TREETEE (f)? _____

○ What is the English for THEFTERA? _____

TURN BACK FOR THE ANSWERS

COVER UP THE LEFT HAND PAGE BEFORE ANSWERING

○ What is the Greek for Sunday? _____

○ What is the Greek for Saturday? _____

○ What is the Greek for Friday? _____

○ What is the Greek for Thursday? _____

○ What is the Greek for Wednesday? _____

○ What is the Greek for Tuesday? _____

○ What is the Greek for Monday? _____

TURN BACK FOR THE ANSWERS

ELEMENTARY GRAMMAR

PLEASE NOTE that in Greek you always use the word 'the' with the days of the week.

For example,

> TUESDAY IS GOOD is EE TREETEE EENAH KALEE

When you want to say   THE MOTHER SEES THE FISH ON
TUESDAY

in Greek you say   EE MEETERA VLEPEE TOH
PSAREE TEEN TREETEE.

In other words, you treat the day of the week as if it were the object of the sentence. However, in sentences such as

> TODAY IS TUESDAY

or

> YESTERDAY WAS MONDAY

You miss out "THE".

Don't worry if you make mistakes. You will be understood.

Now cover up the answers below and translate the following:

(You can write your answers in)

1. EE KEERYAKEE THEN EENAH POTEH EESEEHEE
2. EE PEMTEE EENAH PANDA OREA
3. TOH SAVATOH EENAH EPEESEES KALO
4. SEEMERA EENAH THEFTERA
5. CHTHES EETAN PARASKEVEE
6. OH YOS THELEE TOH PSAREE TEEN TREETEE

The answers are:

1. SUNDAY IS NEVER QUIET
2. THURSDAY IS ALWAYS BEAUTIFUL
3. SATURDAY IS ALSO GOOD
4. TODAY IS MONDAY
5. YESTERDAY WAS FRIDAY
6. THE SON WANTS THE FISH ON TUESDAY

Now cover up the answers below and translate the following:

(You can write your answers in)

1. SUNDAY IS BEAUTIFUL
2. TODAY IS MONDAY
3. YESTERDAY THE BROTHER WAS HERE AND IT WAS TUESDAY
4. AT MIDDAY MOTHER EATS THE FRUIT
5. THE MAN DOES NOT WANT THE MELON ON FRIDAY

The answers are:

1. EE KEERYAKEE EENAH OREA
2. SEEMERA EENAH THEFTERA
3. CHTHES OH ATHELFOS EETAN ETHOH KEE EETAN TREETEE
4. TOH MESSEMEREE EE MEETERA TROEE TOH FROOTOH
5. OH ANDRAS THEN THELEE TOH PEPONEE TEEN PARASKEVEE

Section 5 IN THE RESTAURANT, NUMBERS, TELL-
ING THE TIME

**THINK OF EACH IMAGE IN YOUR MIND'S EYE FOR ABOUT
TEN SECONDS**

○ The Greek for RESTAURANT is RESTORAN (n)
Imagine a group of Greek gods eating in a divine restaurant.

○ The Greek for WAITER is GARSONEE
Imagine asking a waiter, "Have you left the GAS ON, EH?"

○ The Greek for PLATE is PIATOH
Imagine saying, "BE AT HOME, throw plates around."

○ The Greek for KNIFE is MACHEREE*
Imagine saying to your wife, "MY CHERI, I will kill you
with a knife."

○ The Greek for FORK is PEEROONEE
Imagine sticking forks into the PYRENESE Mountains.

○ The Greek for SPOON is COOTALEE
Imagine I COULD TELL YOU about spoons.

○ The Greek for BILL is LORRARYASMOS
Imagine your girlfriend LAURA HAS MOST of the bill.

○ The Greek for MENU is MENU (n)
Imagine Greek gods are reading a menu.

○ The Greek for BOTTLE is BOOKALEE
Imagine you should BOOK EARLY for a bottle in Greece.

○ The Greek for GLASS is POTEEREE
Imagine a POTTERY making glasses.

---

* In this word CH is pronounced more like an H than the CH in LOCH.

YOU CAN WRITE YOUR ANSWERs IN

○ What is the English for POTEEREE? _____

○ What is the English for BOOKALEE? _____

○ What is the English for MENU (n)? _____

○ What is the English for
   LORRARYASMOS? _____

○ What is the English for COOTALEE? _____

○ What is the English for PEEROONEE? _____

○ What is the English for MACHEREE? _____

○ What is the English for PIATOH? _____

○ What is the English for GARSONEE? _____

○ What is the English for RESTORAN (n)? _____

TURN BACK FOR THE ANSWERS

COVER UP THE LEFT HAND PAGE BEFORE
ANSWERING

○ What is the Greek for glass?   _____

○ What is the Greek for bottle?   _____

○ What is the Greek for menu?   _____

○ What is the Greek for bill?   _____

○ What is the Greek for spoon?   _____

○ What is the Greek for fork?   _____

○ What is the Greek for knife?   _____

○ What is the Greek for plate?   _____

○ What is the Greek for waiter?   _____

○ What is the Greek for restaurant?   _____

TURN BACK FOR THE ANSWERS

SOME MORE DESCRIPTIVE WORDS

THINK OF EACH IMAGE IN YOUR MIND'S EYE FOR ABOUT TEN SECONDS

○ The Greek for WET is EERR-ROH
Imagine someone is very wet to be a HERO.

○ The Greek for DRY is KSEROH
Imagine a slave saying, "SIR OH! I am here to dry you."

○ The Greek for OLD is PALYOH
Imagine thinking about an old building "What an old PAL YOU are."

○ The Greek for BIG is MERRALOH*
Imagine someone big going MERRILY about her job.

○ The Greek for SOFT is MALAKOH
Imagine MY LACK O' soft skin is a social handicap.

*Remember the 'RR' is very soft at the back of the throat and sounds as much like a "dirty G" sound as anything.

YOU CAN WRITE YOUR ANSWERS IN

○ What is the English for MALAKOH?   _____

○ What is the English for MERRALOH?   _____

○ What is the English for PALYOH?   _____

○ What is the English for KSEROH?   _____

○ What is the English for EERROH?   _____

TURN BACK FOR THE ANSWERS

124

COVER UP THE LEFT HAND PAGE BEFORE
ANSWERING

○ What is the Greek for soft? _____

○ What is the Greek for big? _____

○ What is the Greek for old? _____

○ What is the Greek for dry? _____

○ What is the Greek for wet? _____

TURN BACK FOR THE ANSWERS

ELEMENTARY GRAMMAR

PLURALS

Plurals are slightly complicated in Greek, but we will give you three rules that will mean that you will be right in most cases.

However, even if you are wrong you will always be understood.

First, the plural of MASCULINE words:

Singular	*Plural*
SKEELOS (dog)	SKELEE (dogs)
ASTAKOS (lobster)	ASTAKEE (lobsters)

In other words, the masculine words end in -EE in the plural.

The word for THE in the masculine plural is EE.

This is the same as the ending of the noun.

So,

OH SKEELOS (the dog)	becomes EE SKEELEE (the dogs).
OH ASTAKOS (the lobster)	becomes EE ASTAKEE (the lobsters).

The adjectives also end accordingly.

For example,

OH LEPTOS SKEELOS (the thin dog) becomes EE LEPTEE SKEELEE (the thin dogs)

Again,

THE THIN DOG IS QUIET is OH LEPTOS SKEELOS EENAH EESEEHOS.

In the plural this is

EE LEPTEE SKEELEE EENAH EESEEHEE (the thin dogs are quiet).

To remember that EE is the masculine ending in the plural, imagine HE men.

Now cover up the answers below and translate the following:

(You can write your answers in)

1. EE KALEE SKEELEE EENAH MIKREE KEH TOH MER-RALOH POTEEREE EENAH GREE

2. EE NE-EE ASTAKEE EENAH KAKEE KEE OH PALYOS TEECHOS EENAH EERR-HOS

3. EE ORE-EE SOLOMEE EENAH EESEEHEE ALAH TOH BOOKALEE EENAH KAKOH

4. EE MIKREE KEEPEE EENAH ORE-EE KEH KSEREE

5. EE MIKREE ATHELFEE EENAH KAKEE KEH TOH COOTALEE EENAH MAVROH

The answers are:

1. THE GOOD DOGS ARE SMALL AND THE BIG GLASS IS GREY

2. THE YOUNG LOBSTERS ARE BAD AND THE OLD WALL IS WET

3. THE BEAUTIFUL SALMON ARE QUIET BUT THE BOT-TLE IS BAD

4. THE SMALL GARDENS ARE BEAUTIFUL AND DRY

5. THE SMALL BROTHERS ARE BAD (or THE SMALL SISTER IS BAD) AND THE SPOON IS BLACK

Now cover up the answers below and translate the following:

(You can write your answers in)

1. THE BAD MEN ARE BIG AND THE SMALL BILLS ARE GOOD AND DRY
   N.B. The plural of ANDRAS is ANDRES.

2. THE SMALL DOGS ARE BEAUTIFUL AND THE RESTAURANT IS VERY QUIET

3. THE SOFT LOBSTERS ARE OLD, BUT THE KNIFE AND THE FORK ARE HERE

4. THE YOUNG BROTHERS ARE GOOD, BUT THE PLATE WAS NEVER GREEN

5. THE BIG WALLS ARE WET, BUT THE MENU IS GOOD

The answers are:

1. EE KAKEE ANDRES EENAH MERRALEE KEE EE MIKREE LORRARYASMEE EENEE KALEE KEE KSEREE

2. EE MIKREE SKEELEE EENAH ORE-EE KEH TOH RESTORAN EENAH POLEE EESEEHOH

3. EE MALAKEE ASTAKEE EENAH PALYEE, ALAH TOH MACHEREE KEH TOH PEEROONEE EENAH ETHOH

4. EE NEEE ATHELFEE EENAH KALEE ALAH TOH PIATOH THEN EETAN POTEH PRASEENOH

5. EE MERRALEE TEECHEE EENAH EERR-REE ALAH TOH MENU EENAH KALOH

128

ELEMENTARY GRAMMAR

Now we will give you the second rule, and this applies to FEMININE plurals.

Singular	*Plural*
RRATA (cat)	RRATES (cats)
ATHELFEE (sister)	ATHELFES (sisters)

In other words, the feminine words end in -ES in the plural.

The word for THE in the feminine plural is EE – as it is for the masculine plurals.

So,

EE FOOSTA (the skirt)   becomes   EE FOOSTES (the skirts).

EE SKALA (the staircase)   becomes   EE SKALES (the staircases).

The adjectives also end accordingly.

For example,

EE MIKREE RRATA (the small cat) becomes EE MIKRES RRATES (the small cats).

EE MALAKEE RRATA EENAH KAKEE (the soft cat is bad) becomes EE MALAKES RRATES EENAH KAKES (the soft cats are bad).

To remember that ES is the feminine ending in the plural, imagine thinking, "YES, girls are pretty."

Now cover up the answers below and translate the following:

(You can write your answers in)

1. EE RRLEEKES MEETERES EENAH KALES KEE EE
   EER-RES KAMARES EENAH MERRALES

2. EE MIKRES RRATES EENAH EESEEHES ALAH EE
   MAVRES FOOSTES EENAH EKEE

3. EE ORE-EES SKALES EENAH KSERES KEE EE
   NICHTES THEN EENAH POTEH KALES

4. EE MERRALES PETALOOTHES EENAH HAZES KEE EE
   ZAKETES EENAH PRASEENES

5. EE KAKES ATHELFES EENAH NE-ES ALAH EE
   EVTHOMATHES EENAH PANDA ORE-ES

The answers are:

1. THE SWEET MOTHERS ARE GOOD AND THE WET
   ROOMS ARE BIG

2. THE SMALL CATS ARE QUIET BUT THE BLACK SKIRTS
   ARE THERE

3. THE BEAUTIFUL STAIRCASES ARE DRY AND THE
   NIGHTS ARE NEVER GOOD

4. THE BIG BUTTERFLIES ARE STUPID AND THE
   JACKETS ARE GREEN

5. THE BAD SISTERS ARE YOUNG BUT THE WEEKS ARE
   ALWAYS BEAUTIFUL

Now cover up the answers below and translate the following:

(You can write your answers in)

1. THE BIG CATS ARE QUIET AND THE RESTAURANT IS ALWAYS DARK

2. THE YOUNG SISTERS ARE BEAUTIFUL TODAY BUT THE GREEN TREE IS DRY

3. THE OLD SKIRTS ARE BIG BUT THE RED BLOUSES ARE SMALL

4. THE YOUNG WOMEN ARE DRY AND THE BIG WALLS ARE BROWN

5. THE SMALL BEES ARE SOFT AND THE BAD HENS ARE HERE

The answers are:

1. EE MERRALES RRATES EENAH EESEEHES KEH TOH RESTORAN EENAH PANDA SKOTEENOH

2. EE NE-ES ATHELFES EENAH ORE-ES SEEMERA ALAH TOH PRASEENOH THENDROH EENAH KSEROH

3. EE PALYES FOOSTES EENAH MERRALES ALAH EE KOKEENES BLOOSES EENAH MIKRES

4. EE NE-ES YEENEKES EENAH KSERES KEE EE MER-RALEE TEECHEE EENAH KAFE

5. EE MIKRES MELEESES EENAH MALAKES KEE EE KAKES KOTES EENAH ETHOH

ELEMENTARY GRAMMAR

Now we will give you the third rule, and this applies to NEUTER plurals.

Singular	*Plural*
PSAREE (fish)	PSARYA (fishes)
PIATOH (plate)	PIATA (plates)

In other words, the neuter words end in -A in the plural.

The word for THE in the neuter plural is TA.

For example,

TOH MACHEREE (the knife) becomes TA MACHERYA (the knives).

TOH POOLEE (the bird)   becomes TA POOLYA (the birds).

The adjectives also end accordingly.

For example,

TOH MERRALOH MACHEREE becomes TA MERRALA (the big knife)   MACHERYA (the big knives).

TOH MIKROH POOLEE becomes TA MIKRA EENAH KAKOH (the small bird POOLYA is bad)   EENAH KAKA (the small birds are bad).

To remember that A is the neuter ending in the plural, imagine thinking, "AH, neutered cats."

PLEASE NOTE

The noun ends with an A, but sometimes with a YA. It does not matter at this stage if you get this wrong. The important rule is to make the neuter word end with an A in the plural.

Now cover up the answers below and translate the following:

(You can write your answers in)

1. TA MERRALA POOLYA EENAH KALA EE KAKA
2. TA MIKRA PSARYA EENAH KAKA KEH MALAKÁ
3. TA OREA PIATA EENAH PALYA KEH KOKEENA
4. TA EESEEHA ARROHRYA EENAH RRLEEKA ALAH TA KOREETSYA THEN EENAH POTEH POLEE EESEEHA
5. TA NEA KOREETSYA EENAH LEPTA KEH MIKRA

The answers are:

1. THE BIG BIRDS ARE GOOD OR BAD
2. THE SMALL FISH(ES) ARE BAD AND SOFT
3. THE BEAUTIFUL PLATES ARE OLD AND RED
4. THE QUIET BOYS ARE SWEET BUT THE GIRLS ARE NEVER VERY QUIET
5. THE YOUNG GIRLS ARE THIN AND SMALL

Now cover up the answers below and translate the following:

(You can write your answers in)

1. THE SMALL GIRLS ARE BEAUTIFUL, BUT THE BIG WAITERS ARE WET

2. THE BIG PLATES ARE DRY, BUT THE HATS ARE ALWAYS OLD

3. THE OLD FORKS ARE WET AND THE SOFT GLASSES ARE BLUE

4. THE BAD MOSQUITOS ARE QUIET TODAY

5. THE SMALL SPOONS ARE SWEET AND DRY AND THE FORKS ARE SMALL

The answers are:

1. TA MIKRA KOREETSYA EENAH OREA ALAH TA MER-RALA GARSONYA EENAH EERR-RA

2. TA MERRALA PIATA EENAH KSERA ALAH TA KAPELA EENAH PANDA PALYA

3. TA PALYA PEEROONYA EENAH EERRA KEH TA MALAKÁ POTEERYA EENAH BLE

4. TA KAKÁ KOONOOPYA EENAH EESEEHA SEEMERA

5. TA MIKRA KOOTALYA EENAH RRLEEKA KEH KSERA KEE TA PEEROONYA EENAH MIKRA

NUMBERS

THINK OF EACH IMAGE IN YOUR MIND'S EYE FOR ABOUT TEN SECONDS

○ The Greek for ONE is ENA
  Imagine ANY one will do.

○ The Greek for TWO is THEEOH
  Imagine THEOdore Roosevelt had two sons.

○ The Greek for THREE is TREEA
  Imagine three on a TREE Away in the distance.

○ The Greek for FOUR is TESERA
  Imagine giving four sons TO SARAH the wife of Isaac.

○ The Greek for FIVE is PENDE
  Imagine a PENTAthlon consists of five events.

○ The Greek for SIX is EXEE
  Imagine no-one looks SEXY at six.

○ The Greek for SEVEN is EFTA
  Imagine seventh Heaven comes AFTER being good.

○ The Greek for EIGHT is OCHTOH
  Imagine an OCTOpus with eight arms.

○ The Greek for NINE is ENYA
  Imagine on average, you have nine pints of blood IN YOU.

○ The Greek for ZERO is MEETHEN
  Imagine if you have zero money, there must be something MISSING.

YOU CAN WRITE YOUR ANSWERS IN

○ What is the English for MEETHEN? _____

○ What is the English for ENYA? _____

○ What is the English for OCHTOH? _____

○ What is the English for EFTA? _____

○ What is the English for EXEE? _____

○ What is the English for PENDE? _____

○ What is the English for TESERA? _____

○ What is the English for TREEA? _____

○ What is the English for THEEOH? _____

○ What is the English for ENA? _____

TURN BACK FOR THE ANSWERS

COVER UP THE LEFT HAND PAGE BEFORE
ANSWERING

○ What is the Greek for zero? _____

○ What is the Greek for nine? _____

○ What is the Greek for eight? _____

○ What is the Greek for seven? _____

○ What is the Greek for six? _____

○ What is the Greek for five? _____

○ What is the Greek for four? _____

○ What is the Greek for three? _____

○ What is the Greek for two? _____

○ What is the Greek for one? _____

TURN BACK FOR THE ANSWERS

Now cover up the answers below and translate the following:

(You can write your answers in)

1. EE THEEOH MERES EENAH MERRALES

2. TA EXEE KOREETSYA THEN EENAH POLEE OREA

3. TOH ENA PALTOH EENAH KAFE ALAH TA THEEOH
   FOOSTANYA EENAH BLE

4. SEEMERA EE MEETERA TROEE OCHTOH STAFEELYA

5. TA EFTA MACHERYA THEN EENAH KAKA

The answers are:

1. THE TWO DAYS ARE BIG

2. THE SIX GIRLS ARE NOT VERY BEAUTIFUL

3. THE ONE COAT IS BROWN BUT THE TWO DRESSES
   ARE BLUE

4. TODAY MOTHER EATS EIGHT GRAPES

5. THE SEVEN KNIVES ARE NOT BAD

Now cover up the answers below and translate the following:

(You can write your answers in)

1. THE THREE SHOES ARE SMALL AND DRY
2. THE FIVE PLATES ARE BIG AND SOFT
3. THE FOUR FORKS ARE GREEN AND SMALL
4. THE SEVEN SKIRTS ARE ALWAYS BLACK
5. THE NINE MONTHS ARE NEVER GOOD

The answers are:

1. TA TREEA PAPOOTSYA EENAH MIKRA KEH KSERA
2. TA PENDE PIATA EENAH MERRALA KEH MALAKA
3. TA TESERA PEEROONYA EENAH PRASEENA KEH MIKRA
4. EE EFTA FOOSTES EENAH PANDA MAVRES
5. EE ENYA MEENES THEN EENAH POTEH KALEE

TELLING THE TIME

The next section will deal with telling the time in Greek. Before you can do so, however, you will need to know a few more words.

THINK OF EACH IMAGE IN YOUR MIND'S EYE FOR ABOUT TEN SECONDS

○ The Greek for TEN is THEKA
Imagine someone who cannot count to TEN is THICKER than me.

○ The Greek for ELEVEN is ENTHEKA
Imagine you get thicker AND THICKER if you cannot count to ELEVEN.

○ The Greek for TWELVE is THOTHEKA
Imagine SO THICK A boy, he cannot count to TWELVE.

○ The Greek for TWENTY is EEKOSEE
Imagine A COSY number is TWENTY.

○ The Greek for TWENTY-FIVE is EEKOSEE PENDE
Imagine TWENTY-FIVE is just TWENTY-FIVE in Greek also – EEKOSEE PENDE.

○ The Greek for QUARTER is TETARTOH
Imagine you have to QUARTER THE TART OH!

○ The Greek for HALF is MEESOH
Imagine they made ME SAW a magician in HALF.

○ The Greek for BUT is PARA
Imagine you enjoy all sports BUT PARAchuting.
(N.B. This BUT is used only for telling the time.)

YOU CAN WRITE YOUR ANSWERS IN

○ What is the English for PARA? _____

○ What is the English for MEESOH? _____

○ What is the English for TETARTOH? _____

○ What is the English for EEKOSEE
   PENDE? _____

○ What is the English for EEKOSEE? _____

○ What is the English for THOTHEKA? _____

○ What is the English for ENTHEKA? _____

○ What is the English for THEKA? _____

TURN BACK FOR THE ANSWERS

COVER UP THE LEFT HAND PAGE BEFORE
ANSWERING

○ What is the Greek for but?   _____

○ What is the Greek for half?   _____

○ What is the Greek for quarter?   _____

○ What is the Greek for twenty-five?   _____

○ What is the Greek for twenty?   _____

○ What is the Greek for twelve?   _____

○ What is the Greek for eleven?   _____

○ What is the Greek for ten?   _____

TURN BACK FOR THE ANSWERS

ELEMENTARY GRAMMAR

TELLING THE TIME

It is very easy to tell the time in Greek.

To ask "WHAT TIME IS IT?" you simply say TEE ORA EENAH? ("what hour is it?")

The usual answer is EENAH . . .

For example, if it is two o'clock the answer would be EENAH THEEOH.

Now, using two as the example:

2.05	is	THEEOH KEH PENDE
2.10	is	THEEOH KEH THEKA
2.15	is	THEEOH KEH TETARTOH
2.20	is	THEEOH KEH EEKOSEE
2.25	is	THEEOH KEH EEKOSEE PENDE

In other words, you say:

TWO AND FIVE, TWO AND TEN, TWO AND QUARTER, TWO AND TWENTY, etc.

To say 2.30, you say TWO AND HALF.

1.45	is	THEEOH PARA TETARTOH
1.50	is	THEEOH PARA THEKA
1.55	is	THEEOH PARA PENDE

In other words, to say 1.50 you say TWO BUT TEN

1.40 is TWO BUT TWENTY, etc.

Note, that only when telling the time:

instead of one (ENA), three (TREEA), four (TESERA)
and MEESOH (half) you say MEEA, TREES, TESSERES and MEESSEE.

For example,

1.15	is	MEEA KEH TETARTOH
2.30	is	THEEOH KEH MEESSEE
3.05	is	TREES KEH PENDE
4.20	is	TESSERES KEH EEKOSEE

Now cover up the answers below and translate the following:

(You can write your answers in)

1. EENAH OCHTOH PARA EEKOSEE
2. EENAH EXEE KEH MEESSEE
3. EENAH TREES PARA TETARTOH
4. EENAH ENTHEKA KEH PENDE
5. EENAH THOTHEKA KEH TETARTOH

The answers are:

1. IT IS TWENTY TO EIGHT
2. IT IS SIX THIRTY
3. IT IS A QUARTER TO THREE
4. IT IS FIVE PAST ELEVEN
5. IT IS QUARTER PAST TWELVE

Now cover up the answers below and translate the following:

(You can write your answers in)

1. IT IS HALF PAST SIX
2. IT IS QUARTER TO SEVEN
3. IT IS FIVE PAST NINE
4. IT IS TEN TO FOUR
5. IT IS TWENTY-FIVE PAST ONE

The answers are:

1. EENAH EXEE KEH MEESSEE
2. EENAH EFTA PARA TETARTOH
3. EENAH ENYA KEH PENDE
4. EENAH TESSERES PARA THEKA
5. EENAH MEEA KEH EEKOSEE PENDE

Section 6   FOOD AND DRINK

THINK OF EACH IMAGE IN YOUR MIND'S EYE FOR ABOUT TEN SECONDS

○ The Greek for SOUP is SOOPA
Imagine you prepare soup fit for a Greek god.

○ The Greek for RICE is REEZEE
Imagine Greek gods throw rice at each other.

○ The Greek for TOMATO is DOMATA
Imagine Greek gods eating tomatoes.

○ The Greek for CHEESE is TEEREE
Imagine being in tears – TEARY – after eating Greek cheese.

○ The Greek for EGG is AVRROH
Imagine I THROW eggs often.

○ The Greek for COFFEE is KAFES (m)
Imagine you drink coffee in CAFES.

○ The Greek for TEA is TSAEE
Imagine you SIGH for a cup of tea.

○ The Greek for WATER is NEROH
Imagine the Emperor NERO drinking water.

○ The Greek for WINE is KRASEE
Imagine Greek wine tastes GRASSY.

○ The Greek for SUGAR is ZACHAREE
Imagine you always take SACCHARINE instead of sugar.

YOU CAN WRITE YOUR ANSWERS IN

○ What is the English for ZACHAREE? _____

○ What is the English for KRASEE? _____

○ What is the English for NEROH? _____

○ What is the English for TSAEE? _____

○ What is the English for KAFES (m)? _____

○ What is the English for AVRROH? _____

○ What is the English for TEEREE? _____

○ What is the English for DOMATA? _____

○ What is the English for REEZEE? _____

○ What is the English for SOOPA? _____

TURN BACK FOR THE ANSWERS

COVER UP THE LEFT HAND PAGE BEFORE ANSWERING

○ What is the Greek for sugar?   _____

○ What is the Greek for wine?   _____

○ What is the Greek for water?   _____

○ What is the Greek for tea?   _____

○ What is the Greek for coffee?   _____

○ What is the Greek for egg?   _____

○ What is the Greek for cheese?   _____

○ What is the Greek for tomato?   _____

○ What is the Greek for rice?   _____

○ What is the Greek for soup?   _____

TURN BACK FOR THE ANSWERS

SOME USEFUL PLACE WORDS

THINK OF EACH IMAGE IN YOUR MIND'S EYE FOR ABOUT TEN SECONDS

○ The Greek for BEFORE is PREEN
  Imagine a bird PREENS itself before breakfast.

○ The Greek for AFTER is META
  Imagine you are happy after you MET HER.

○ The Greek for BEHIND is PEESOH
  Imagine the Leaning Tower of PISA behind you.

○ The Greek for ON is PANOH
  Imagine a PAN O' water on your head.

○ The Greek for UNDER is CATOH
  Imagine a CAT O' nine tails under the table.

○ The Greek for FROM is APOH
  Imagine a worm eating its way from an APPLE to a pear.

○ The Greek for IN(SIDE) is MESA
  Imagine it is MESSY in your room.

○ The Greek for OUT(SIDE) is EXOH
  Imagine putting an EXOcet missile outside of the house.

YOU CAN WRITE YOUR ANSWERS IN

○ What is the English for EXOH? _____

○ What is the English for MESA? _____

○ What is the English for APOH? _____

○ What is the English for CATOH? _____

○ What is the English for PANOH? _____

○ What is the English for PEESOH? _____

○ What is the English for META? _____

○ What is the English for PREEN? _____

TURN BACK FOR THE ANSWERS

COVER UP THE LEFT HAND PAGE BEFORE
ANSWERING

○ What is the Greek for out(side)? _____

○ What is the Greek for in(side)? _____

○ What is the Greek for from? _____

○ What is the Greek for under? _____

○ What is the Greek for on? _____

○ What is the Greek for behind? _____

○ What is the Greek for after? _____

○ What is the Greek for before? _____

TURN BACK FOR THE ANSWERS

Note: PANOH also mean UP.

ELEMENTARY GRAMMAR

You have just learned eight words that are place words.

As in English, place words (prepositions) are a bit tricky to use. However, we will give you some rules to make it easy.

The first rule is that to say
>THE DOG IS UNDER THE TABLE

you say

>OH SKEELOS EENAH CATOH APOH TOH TRAPEZEE.

In other words APOH follows the word for UNDER.

>To say   THE CAT IS BEHIND THE STAIRCASE
>
>you say   EE RRATA EENAH PEESOH APOH TEEN SKALA.

Again, the word APOH follows the word for BEHIND.

The words CATOH (under), PEESOH (behind), EXOH (out), PREEN (before), META (after) are always followed by APOH in sentences such as those that you have just seen.

So,

THE GIRL IS BEHIND THE CURTAIN	is TOH KOREETSEE EENAH PEESOH APOH TEEN COORTEENA.
THE BOY IS AFTER THE FATHER	is TOH ARROHREE EENAH META APOH TON PATERA.
THE CHAIR IS OUT OF THE ROOM	is EE KAREKLA EENAH EXOH APOH TEEN KAMARA.

The second rule is that following the preposition, you use TON, TEEN, TOH for the word THE – depending on the gender of the word following.

So,

THE DOG IS UNDER THE TABLE	is OH SKEELOS EENAH CATOH APOH TOH TRAPEEZEE.
THE DOG IS UNDER THE CAT	is OH SKEELOS EENAH CATOH APOH TEEN RRATA.

Now cover up the answers below and translate the following:

(You can write your answers in)

1. TOH AVRROH EENAH CATOH APOH TOH TRAPEZEE KEH TOH AVRROH EENAH PEESOH APOH TOH PIATOH

2. EE TREETEE EENAH META APOH TEEN THEFTERA

3. EE PEMTEE EENAH PREEN APOH TOH SAVATOH

4. TOH NEROH EENAH EXOH APOH TOH BOOKALEE ALAH OH KAFES EENAH META APOH TOH KRASEE

5. TOH RAFEE EENAH PEESOH APOH TOH SIRTAREE KEH TOH MALAKOH TEEREE EENAH PREEN APOH TEEN SOOPA

The answers are:

1. THE EGG IS UNDER THE TABLE AND THE EGG IS BEHIND THE PLATE

2. TUESDAY IS AFTER MONDAY

3. THURSDAY IS BEFORE SATURDAY

4. THE WATER IS OUTSIDE THE BOTTLE BUT THE COFFEE IS AFTER THE WINE

5. THE SHELF IS BEHIND THE DRAWER AND THE SOFT CHEESE IS BEFORE THE SOUP

Now cover up the answers below and translate the following:

(You can write your answers in)

1. THE WAITER IS OUTSIDE THE RESTAURANT AND THE MAN IS BEFORE THE DOOR

2. THE KNIFE IS UNDER THE PLATE AND THE BOTTLES ARE ALWAYS OUTSIDE THE ROOM

3. THE GIRL IS BEHIND THE BED, BUT THE BLUE FORKS ARE UNDER THE STAIRCASE

4. THE MOTHER EATS AFTER THE DAUGHTER AND THE BROTHER IS BEHIND THE GARDEN

5. THE BOY WANTS THE TOMATO BEFORE THE SOUP AND THE CHEESE AFTER THE EGGS

The answers are:

1. TOH GARSONEE EENAH EXOH APOH TOH RESTAU-RAN KEE OH ANDRAS EENAH PREEN APOH TEEN PORTA

2. TOH MACHEREE EENAH CATOH APOH TOH PIATOH KEH TA BOOKALYA EENAH PANDA EXOH APOH TEEN KAMARA

3. TOH KOREETSEE EENAH PEESOH APOH TOH KREVATEE, ALAH TA BLE PEEROONYA EENAH KATOH APOH TEEN SCALA

4. EE MEETERA TROEE META APOH TEEN KOREE KEE OH ATHELFOS EENAH PEESOH APOH TON KEEPO

5. TOH ARROHREE THELEE TEEN DOMATA PREEN APOH TEEN SOOPA KEH TOH TEEREE META APOH TA AVRRA

156

MORE FOOD WORDS

THINK OF EACH IMAGE IN YOUR MIND'S EYE FOR ABOUT TEN SECONDS

○ The Greek for BREAD is PSOMEE
Imagine you SAW ME eating bread.

○ The Greek for MEAT is KREAS (n)
Imagine you always eat CRESS with meat.

○ The Greek for MILK is RRALA (n)
Imagine a milk RALLY to promote milk sales.

○ The Greek for SALAD is SALATA
Imagine a Greek god ordering a salad.

○ The Greek for CAKE is RRLEEKOH
Imagine you always eat LEEK ON cakes.
N.B. RRLEEKOH is also the word for sweet.

○ The Greek for BEER is BEERA
Imagine Greek gods getting drunk on beer.

○ The Greek for BANANA is BANANA
Imagine a Greek god eating a banana.

○ The Greek for OLIVE is ELYA
Imagine you are so ILL YOU drink olive oil.

○ The Greek for LETTUCE is MAROOLEE
Imagine that MY RULE is that I always eat lettuce.

○ The Greek for POTATO is PATATA
Imagine a Greek god mashing potatoes.

YOU CAN WRITE YOUR ANSWERS IN

○ What is the English for PATATA? _____

○ What is the English for MAROOLEE? _____

○ What is the English for ELYA? _____

○ What is the English for BANANA? _____

○ What is the English for BEERA? _____

○ What is the English for RRLEEKOH? _____

○ What is the English for SALATA? _____

○ What is the English for RRALA (n)? _____

○ What is the English for KREAS (n)? _____

○ What is the English for PSOMEE? _____

TURN BACK FOR THE ANSWERS

COVER UP THE LEFT HAND PAGE BEFORE ANSWERING

○ What is the Greek for potato?   _____

○ What is the Greek for lettuce?   _____

○ What is the Greek for olive?   _____

○ What is the Greek for banana?   _____

○ What is the Greek for beer?   _____

○ What is the Greek for cake?   _____

○ What is the Greek for salad?   _____

○ What is the Greek for milk?   _____

○ What is the Greek for meat?   _____

○ What is the Greek for bread?   _____

TURN BACK FOR THE ANSWERS

FURTHER FOOD WORDS

THINK OF EACH IMAGE IN YOUR MIND'S EYE FOR ABOUT TEN SECONDS

○ The Greek for SPINACH is SPANAKEE
Imagine you get a SPANKING because you will not eat your spinach.

○ The Greek for PEA is ARAKAS (m)
Imagine you make A RACKET eating peas.

○ The Greek for BEAN is FASOLEE
Imagine beans covering the FAST LANE of the motorway.

○ The Greek for CUCUMBER is ANGOOREE
Imagine being ANGRY because you are served with rotten cucumber.

○ The Greek for OIL is LATHEE
Imagine shouting, "LASSIE come home and I'll feed you your favourite oil."

○ The Greek for HAM is ZAMBON (n)
Imagine putting JAM ON ham.

○ The Greek for CHOCOLATE is SOKOLATA
Imagine chocolate fit for Greek gods.

○ The Greek for STARTER is MEZES (m)
Imagine giving your MRS a starter.

○ The Greek for BISCUIT is BISKOTOH
Imagine feeding biscuits to the Greek gods.

○ The Greek for VINEGAR is XITHEE
Imagine you SEE THE vinegar.

YOU CAN WRITE YOUR ANSWERS IN

○ What is the English for XITHEE? _____

○ What is the English for BISKOTOH? _____

○ What is the English for MEZES (m) _____

○ What is the English for SOKOLATA? _____

○ What is the English for ZAMBON (n)? _____

○ What is the English for LATHEE? _____

○ What is the English for ANGOOREE? _____

○ What is the English for FASOLEE? _____

○ What is the English for ARAKAS (m)? _____

○ What is the English for SPANAKEE? _____

TURN BACK FOR THE ANSWERS

COVER UP THE LEFT HAND PAGE BEFORE ANSWERING

○ What is the Greek for vinegar? _____

○ What is the Greek for biscuit? _____

○ What is the Greek for starter? _____

○ What is the Greek for chocolate? _____

○ What is the Greek for ham? _____

○ What is the Greek for oil? _____

○ What is the Greek for cucumber? _____

○ What is the Greek for bean? _____

○ What is the Greek for pea? _____

○ What is the Greek for spinach? _____

TURN BACK FOR THE ANSWERS

Note: Another word for PEA is BEEZELEE.

ELEMENTARY GRAMMAR

When you want to say:

THE TOMATOES ARE FROM THE GARDEN

you simply say:

EE DOMATES EENAH APOH TON KEEPO.

So, APOH is used alone but, again depending on the gender of the word following it, you use TON (m), TEEN (f) OR TOH (n) for the word THE.

For example, to say:

THE GIRL EATS FROM THE SOUP

You say

TOH KOREETSEE TROEE APOH TEEN SOOPA.

Now, when you want to say:

THE RICE IS ON THE TABLE

you say

TOH REEZEE EENAH PANOH STOH TRAPEZEE

or:

THE COFFEE IS IN THE GLASS

you say

OH KAFES EENAH MESA STOH POTEEREE.

So, this is the THIRD rule:

MESA (in) and PANOH (on) are always followed by STOH in sentences such as those above.

However, depending on the gender of the word following PANOH and MESA, you use STON (m), STEEN (f) or STOH (n).
So you put the letter "S" in front of TON, TEEN or TOH.

THE CHEESE IS ON THE PLATE	is	TOH TEEREE EENAH PANOH STOH PIATOH
THE WINE IS IN THE BOTTLE	is	TOH KRASEE EENAH MESA STOH BOOKALEE
THE MOTHER IS IN THE GARDEN	is	EE MEETERA EENAH MESA STON KEEPO
THE HAT IS ON THE CHAIR	is	TOH KAPELOH EENAH PANOH STEEN KAREKLA

Now cover up the answers below and translate the following:

(You can write your answers in)

1. TOH REEZEE EENAH PANOH STOH TRAPEZEE KEE EE PATATES EENAH MESA STOH BISKOTOH

2. EE YEENEKA EENAH MESA STON KEEPO KEH TOH XITHEE EENAH MESA STOH LATHEE

3. EE SOOPA EENAH MESA STOH PIATOH ALAH TOH SPANAKE EENAH APOH TON KEEPO

4. TOH COOTALEE EENAH MESA STEEN ZACHAREE KEE EE BEERA EENAH PANOH STOH NEROH

5. TOH LATHEE EENAH PANOH STEEN KOOZEENA ALAH EE ELYES EENAH APOH TA THENDRA

The answers are:

1. THE RICE IS ON THE TABLE AND THE POTATOES ARE IN THE BISCUIT

2. THE WOMAN IS IN THE GARDEN AND THE VINEGAR IS IN THE OIL

3. THE SOUP IS IN THE PLATE BUT THE SPINACH IS FROM THE GARDEN

4. THE SPOON IS IN THE SUGAR AND THE BEER IS ON THE WATER

5. THE OIL IS ON THE COOKER BUT THE OLIVES ARE FROM THE TREES

Now cover up the answers below and translate the following:

(You can write your answers in)

1. THE POTATOES ARE FROM THE GARDEN BUT THE CUCUMBER IS FROM THE RESTAURANT

2. THE BEER IS IN THE GLASS AND THE HAM IS ON THE PLATE

3. THE WINE IS IN THE BOTTLE AND THE BEANS ARE IN THE SOUP

4. THE BREAD IS ON THE TABLE BUT THE CHOCOLATE IS IN THE BISCUIT

5. THE MAN IS ON THE CHAIR AND THE STARTER IS IN THE VINEGAR

The answers are:

1. EE PATATES EENAH APOH TON KEEPO ALAH TOH ANGOOREE EENAH APOH TOH RESTORAN

2. EE BEERA EENAH MESA STOH POTEEREE KEH TOH ZAMBON EENAH PANOH STOH PIATOH

3. TOH KRASEE EENAH MESA STOH BOOKALEE KEH TA FASOLYA EENAH MESA STEEN SOOPA

4. TOH PSOMEE EENAH PANOH STOH TRAPEZEE ALAH EE SOKOLATA EENAH MESA STOH BISKOTOH

5. OH ANDRAS EENAH PANOH STEEN KAREKLA KEE OH MEZES EENAH MESA STOH XITHEE

SOME MORE DESCRIPTIVE WORDS

THINK OF EACH IMAGE IN YOUR MIND'S EYE FOR ABOUT TEN SECONDS

○ The Greek for TALL is PSEELOH
Imagine when you are tall you cannot SEE LOW things.

○ The Greek for DIRTY is VROMEEKOH
Imagine Mr GROMYKO, the Russian statesman, looking dirty.

○ The Greek for RIGHT (correct) is SOSTOH
Imagine you need SAUCE TO make the meal taste right.

○ The Greek for WRONG is LATHOS (n)
Imagine in Greece they LASH US if we are wrong.
N.B. LATHOS means MISTAKE and WRONG.

○ The Greek for ANGRY is THEEMOMENOH
Imagine asking, "Does THE MUMMY KNOW that I am angry?"

○ The Greek for FIRST is PROTOH
Imagine the first thing an inventor does is to make a PROTOtype.

○ The Greek for LAST is TELEFTEOH
Imagine the last person in has to go to THE LEFT, HEY HO!

○ The Greek for SECOND is THEFTEROH
Imagine in Greek, Monday – THEFTERA – is the second day of the week.

○ The Greek for MIDDLE is MESSEHOH
Imagine a MESSY HOLE in the middle of the floor.

○ The Greek for OPEN is ANEECHTOH
Imagine I NEED TO open a window.

○ The Greek for CLOSED is KLEESTOH
Imagine a Chinaman asking "PLEASE TO close door".

YOU CAN WRITE YOUR ANSWERS IN

○ What is the English for KLEESTOH? _____

○ What is the English for ANEECHTOH? _____

○ What is the English for MESSEHOH? _____

○ What is the English for THEFTEROH? _____

○ What is the English for TELEFTEOH? _____

○ What is the English for PROTOH? _____

○ What is the English for
THEEMOMENOH? _____

○ What is the English for LATHOS (n)? _____

○ What is the English for SOSTOH? _____

○ What is the English for VROMEEKOH? _____

○ What is the English for PSEELOH? _____

TURN BACK FOR THE ANSWERS

COVER UP THE LEFT HAND PAGE BEFORE ANSWERING

○ What is the Greek for closed? _____

○ What is the Greek for open? _____

○ What is the Greek for middle? _____

○ What is the Greek for second? _____

○ What is the Greek for last? _____

○ What is the Greek for first? _____

○ What is the Greek for angry? _____

○ What is the Greek for wrong? _____

○ What is the Greek for right (correct)? _____

○ What is the Greek for dirty? _____

○ What is the Greek for tall? _____

TURN BACK FOR THE ANSWERS

Now cover up the answers below the translate the following:

(You can write your answers in)

1. TOH TELEFTEOH LATHOS EETAN MERRALOH

2. TOH PSEELOH THENDROH EENAH MESA STON PRA-
SEENO KEEPO

3. OH SOSTOS LORRARYASMOS EENAH KALOS

4. EE THEEMOMENEE YEENEKA TROEE TOH KAFE
BISKOTOH KEH TOH PROTOH ANGOOREE

5. EE MESSEHA MERA EENAH EE TETARTEE

The answers are:

1. THE LAST MISTAKE WAS BIG

2. THE TALL TREE IS IN THE GREEN GARDEN

3. THE CORRECT BILL IS GOOD

4. THE ANGRY WOMAN EATS THE BROWN BISCUIT AND
THE FIRST CUCUMBER

5. THE MIDDLE DAY IS WEDNESDAY

Now cover up the answers below and translate the following:

(You can write your answers in)

1. THE FIRST RESTAURANT WAS OPEN BUT THE LAST RESTAURANT WAS OLD

2. THE BOY ALWAYS EATS THE LAST CHOCOLATE

3. THE YOUNG GIRL SEES THE TALL SPINACH

4. THE WINE IS IN THE BEAUTIFUL, CLOSED BOTTLE

5. THE RED BEANS ARE DIRTY AND THE MOTHER IS ANGRY

The answers are:

1. TOH PROTOH RESTORAN EETAN ANEECHTOH ALAH TOH TELEFTEOH RESTORAN EETAN PALYO

2. TOH ARROHREE PANDA TROEE TEEN TELEFTEA SOKOLATA

3. TOH NEO KOREETSEE VLEPEE TOH PSEELOH SPANAKEE

4. TOH KRASEE EENAH MESA STOH OREOH, KLEESTOH BOOKALEE

5. TA KOKEENA FASOLYA EENAH VROMEEKA KEE EE MEETERA EENAH THEEMOMENEE

Section 7 SHOPPING AND BUSINESS WORDS

THINK OF EACH IMAGE IN YOUR MIND'S EYE FOR ABOUT TEN SECONDS

○ The Greek for BOSS is AFENDEEKOH
Imagine your boss often OFFENDS THE CO-workers.

○ The Greek for JOB (work) is THOOLYA
Imagine saying, "I will FOOL YOU if you don't give me a job."

○ The Greek for SALARY is MISTHOS
Imagine telling your employer, "You will MISS US if you don't give us a salary."

○ The Greek for MONEY is LEFTA (n plural)
Imagine your relative LEFT A lot of money.

○ The Greek for CHEQUE is EPEETAYEE (f)
Imagine saying, "I PITY YOU if you want a cheque from me."

○ The Greek for OFFICE is RR-RAFEEOH
Imagine eating RAVIOLI in your office.

○ The Greek for SHOP is KATASTEEMA (n)
Imagine a CATASTROPHE occurring while you are in your local shop.

○ The Greek for MARKET is ARRORA
Imagine you hear A ROAR As loud as a lion when you walk through a market.

○ The Greek for SALESMAN is POLEETEES (m)
Imagine POLITICIANS are really failed salesmen.

○ The Greek for ORGANISATION is OR-RRANOSEE
Imagine being told you can climb high in your organisation if you have a good ear OR A NOSE! SEE?

YOU CAN WRITE YOUR ANSWERS IN

○ What is the English for OR-RRANOSEE? _____

○ What is the English for POLEETEES (m)? _____

○ What is the English for ARRORA? _____

○ What is the English for KATASTEEMA (n)? _____

○ What is the English for RR-RAFEEOH? _____

○ What is the English for EPEETAYEE (f)? _____

○ What is the English for LEFTA (n plural)? _____

○ What is the English for MISTHOS? _____

○ What is the English for THOOLYA? _____

○ What is the English for AFENDEEKOH? _____

TURN BACK FOR THE ANSWERS

COVER UP THE LEFT HAND PAGE BEFORE
ANSWERING

○ What is the Greek for organisation?   _____

○ What is the Greek for salesman?   _____

○ What is the Greek for market?   _____

○ What is the Greek for shop?   _____

○ What is the Greek for office?   _____

○ What is the Greek for cheque?   _____

○ What is the Greek for money?   _____

○ What is the Greek for salary?   _____

○ What is the Greek for job (work)?   _____

○ What is the Greek for boss?   _____

TURN BACK FOR THE ANSWERS

NAMES OF SHOPS

THINK OF EACH IMAGE IN YOUR MIND'S EYE FOR ABOUT TEN SECONDS

○ The Greek for BARBER'S SHOP is KOOREEOH
Imagine some people make their CAREERS in a barber's shop.

○ The Greek for CHEMIST'S SHOP is FARMAKEEOH
Imagine the PHARMACY at your local chemist's shop.

○ The Greek for LAUNDERETTE is PLEENDEEREEOH
Imagine you BLEED HER EAR HOLE in a launderette.

○ The Greek for SUPERMARKET is SUPERMARKET
Imagine Greek gods in a supermarket.

○ The Greek for BAKERY is FOORNOS
Imagine a FURNACE in a bakery.

○ The Greek for BUTCHER'S SHOP is HASAPEEKOH
Imagine your butcher always HAS A PEEK OH! when you go past.

○ The Greek for GROCER'S SHOP is BAKALEEKOH
Imagine your grocer tells you "BACK A LEEK OH! for good value".

○ The Greek for KIOSK is PEREEPTEROH
Imagine kiosks on the PERIMETER of a town.

○ The Greek for CASH DESK is TAMEEOH
Imagine saying to a sales girl, "Bring your cash desk TO ME OH!"

○ The Greek for LADIES HAIRDRESSER is KOMOTEEREEOH
Imagine you COMANDEER a ladies' hairdresser.

YOU CAN WRITE YOUR ANSWERS IN

○ What is the English for
  KOMOTEEREEOH? _____

○ What is the English for TAMEEOH? _____

○ What is the English for PEREEPTEROH? _____

○ What is the English for BAKALEEKOH? _____

○ What is the English for HASAPEEKOH? _____

○ What is the English for FOORNOS? _____

○ What is the English for SUPERMARKET? _____

○ What is the English for
  PLEENDEEREEOH? _____

○ What is the English for FARMAKEEOH? _____

○ What is the English for KOOREEOH? _____

TURN BACK FOR THE ANSWERS

COVER UP THE LEFT HAND PAGE BEFORE
ANSWERING

○ What is the Greek for ladies hairdresser? _____

○ What is the Greek for cash desk? _____

○ What is the Greek for kiosk? _____

○ What is the Greek for grocer's shop? _____

○ What is the Greek for butcher's shop? _____

○ What is the Greek for bakery? _____

○ What is the Greek for supermarket? _____

○ What is the Greek for launderette? _____

○ What is the Greek for chemist's shop? _____

○ What is the Greek for barber's shop? _____

TURN BACK FOR THE ANSWERS

PERSONAL WORDS

THINK OF EACH IMAGE IN YOUR MIND'S EYE FOR ABOUT TEN SECONDS

○ The Greek for MY is MOO
   Imagine my cow going MOO.

○ The Greek for YOUR (singular) is SOO
   Imagine you SUE your lawyer.

○ The Greek for OUR is MAS
   Imagine our priest saying MASS.

○ The Greek for YOUR (plural) is SAS
   Imagine your friends live in SASkatoon in Canada.

YOU CAN WRITE YOUR ANSWERS IN

○ What is the English for SAS?   _____

○ What is the English for MAS?   _____

○ What is the English for SOO?   _____

○ What is the English for MOO?   _____

TURN BACK FOR THE ANSWERS

184

COVER UP THE LEFT HAND PAGE BEFORE
ANSWERING

○ What is the Greek for your (plural)? _____

○ What is the Greek for our? _____

○ What is the Greek for your (singular)? _____

○ What is the Greek for my? _____

TURN BACK FOR THE ANSWERS

ELEMENTARY GRAMMAR

In Greek, to say MY DOG IS BLACK you say OH SKEELOS MOO EENAH MAVROS.

To say MY BOSS IS BAD you say TOH AFENDEEKOH MOO EENAH KAKOH.

Now, in order to say

YOUR ROOM IS BIG

you say EE KAMARA SOO EENAH MERRALEE

or to say

YOUR SKIRT IS OLD

you say EE FOOSTA SOO EENAH PALYA.

This is so if you are talking to one person.

In the plural, when you want to say

OUR CATS ARE GOOD

you say

EE RRATES MAS EENAH KALES

or to say

OUR BREAD IS DRY

you say

TOH PSOMEE MAS EENAH KSEROH.

Where you are talking to many people, in order to say

YOUR FRUITS ARE DRY

you say

TA FROOTA SAS EENAH KSERA

or to say

YOUR POTATOES ARE SOFT

you say

EE PATATES SAS EENAH MALAKES.

Now cover up the answers below and translate the following:

(You can write your answers in)

1. TA STAFEELYA MOO EENAH OREA KEH TOH KOO-REEOH SOO EENAH VROMEEKOH

2. TA PAPOOTSYA MAS EENAH PALYA ALAH TOH TAMEEOH EENAH KSEROH

3. EE ATHELFEE SOO EENAH KALEE KEE OH ATHEL-FOS MOO EENAH MALAKOS

4. EE SKEELEE SAS EENAH VROMEEKEE KEE OH FOOR-NOS MAS EENAH ANEECHTOS

5. TOH PEPONEE EENAH MIKROH KEH TOH BAKALEE-KOH SAS EENAH KLEESTOH

The answers are:

1. MY GRAPES ARE BEAUTIFUL AND YOUR BARBER'S SHOP IS DIRTY

2. OUR SHOES ARE OLD BUT THE CASH DESK IS DRY

3. YOUR SISTER IS GOOD AND MY BROTHER IS SOFT

4. YOUR DOGS ARE DIRTY AND OUR BAKERY IS OPEN

5. THE MELON IS SMALL AND YOUR GROCER'S SHOP IS CLOSED

Now cover up the answers below and translate the following:

(You can write your answers in)

1. MY SKIRT IS SMALL AND OUR SHOP IS CLOSED
2. OUR BED IS BIG BUT MY JOB IS GOOD
3. OUR FIGS ARE SWEET AND YOUR (S.) SALARY IS BAD
4. YOUR MOTHER (S.) IS YOUNG AND MY KIOSK IS BIG
5. YOUR (PL.) ROOMS ARE WET BUT YOUR (PL.) MARKET IS OPEN

The answers are:

1. EE FOOSTA MOO EENAH MIKREE KEH TOH KATAS-
   TEEMA MAS EENAH KLEESTOH
2. TOH KREVATEE MAS EENAH MERRALOH ALAH EE
   THOOLYA MOO EENAH KALEE
3. TA SEEKAH MAS EENAH RRLEEKAH KEE OH
   MISTHOS SOO EENAH KAKOS
4. EE MEETERA SOO EENAH NEA KEH TOH PEREEP-
   TEROH MOO EENAH MERRALOH
5. EE KAMARES SAS EENAH EERR-RES ALAH EE
   ARRORA SAS EENAH ANEECHTEE

188

MORE FOOD WORDS

THINK OF EACH IMAGE IN YOUR MIND'S EYE FOR ABOUT TEN SECONDS

○ The Greek for GARLIC is SKORTHOH
Imagine good footballers can still SCORE THOUGH they eat garlic.

○ The Greek for TUNA FISH is TONOS
Imagine TONS of tuna fish.

○ The Greek for LAMB is ARNEE
Imagine the famous golfer ARNIE Palmer hitting a lamb with his golf club.

○ The Greek for PORK is HEEREENOH
Imagine a campaign with the slogan "HERRING NO – pork yes!"

○ The Greek for FILLET STEAK is FEELETOH
Imagine Greek gods eating fillet steak.

○ The Greek for VEAL is MOSCHAREE
Imagine you MUST HURRY to eat your veal.

○ The Greek for CELERY is SELEENOH
Imagine you would be SILLY NOW to eat sticks of celery.

○ The Greek for ICE CREAM is PARROTOH
Imagine a PARROT eating ice cream.

○ The Greek for CREAM is KREMA
Imagine eating cream at a CREMAtorium.

○ The Greek for LEMONADE is LEMONATHA
Imagine Greek gods drinking lemonade.

YOU CAN WRITE YOUR ANSWERS IN

○ What is the English for LEMONATHA? _____

○ What is the English for KREMA? _____

○ What is the English for PARROTOH? _____

○ What is the English for SELEENOH? _____

○ What is the English for MOSCHAREE? _____

○ What is the English for FEELETOH? _____

○ What is the English for HEEREENOH? _____

○ What is the English for ARNEE? _____

○ What is the English for TONOS? _____

○ What is the English for SKORTHOH? _____

TURN BACK FOR THE ANSWERS

COVER UP THE LEFT HAND PAGE BEFORE
ANSWERING

○ What is the Greek for lemonade? _____

○ What is the Greek for cream? _____

○ What is the Greek for ice cream? _____

○ What is the Greek for celery? _____

○ What is the Greek for veal? _____

○ What is the Greek for fillet steak? _____

○ What is the Greek for pork? _____

○ What is the Greek for lamb? _____

○ What is the Greek for tuna fish? _____

○ What is the Greek for garlic? _____

TURN BACK FOR THE ANSWERS

MORE PERSONAL WORDS

THINK OF EACH IMAGE IN YOUR MIND'S EYE FOR ABOUT TEN SECONDS

○ The Greek for HIS is TOO
Imagine his hat is TOO small.

○ The Greek for HER is TEES
Imagine her mother is a TEASE.

○ The Greek for ITS is TOO
Imagine its hat is TOO small.

○ The Greek for THEIR is TOOS
Imagine their family climbs the stairs in TWOS.

YOU CAN WRITE YOUR ANSWERS IN

○ What is the English for TOOS? _____

○ What is the English for TOO? _____

○ What is the English for TEES? _____

○ What is the English for TOO? _____

TURN BACK FOR THE ANSWERS

COVER UP THE LEFT HAND PAGE BEFORE
ANSWERING

○ What is the Greek for their? _____

○ What is the Greek for its? _____

○ What is the Greek for her? _____

○ What is the Greek for his? _____

TURN BACK FOR THE ANSWERS

ELEMENTARY GRAMMAR

If you want to say

    HIS CAT IS GOOD

you say

    EE RRATA TOO EENAH KALEE

or to say

    HIS HAT IS SMALL

you say

    TOH KAPELOH TOO EENAH MIKROH.

If you now want to say

    HER ROOM IS WET

you say

    EE KAMARA TEES EENAH EERR-REE

If you now want to say

    HER APPLES ARE BIG

you say

    TA MEELA TEES EENAH MERRALA.

Finally, if you want to say

    ITS GARDEN IS BIG

you say

    OH KEEPOS TOO EENAH MERRALOS

or to say

    ITS WINE IS GOOD

you say

    TOH KRASEE TOO EENAH KALOH.

Note, then, that TOO is used for both HIS and ITS; that is, both for masculine and neuter.

For plurals, if you want to say

    THEIR TOMATOES ARE SWEET

you say

    EE DOMATES TOOS EENAH RRLEEKES

or to say

    THEIR GARDEN IS BEAUTIFUL

you say

    OH KEEPOS TOOS EENAH OREOS.

Now cover up the answers below and translate the following:

(You can write your answers in)

1. EE DOMATES TOO EENAH VROMEEKES KEH TOH
   AFENDEEKOH TOO THELEE HEEREENOH

2. OH KAFES TEES EENAH RRLEEKOS KEH TOH ARNEE
   TEES ECHEE SELEENOH

3. EE ATHELFES TOOS EENAH NEES ALAH EE
   THOOLYES TOOS EENAH VROMEEKES

4. EE RRATA TOO EENAH MIKREE ALAH TROEE MOS-
   CHAREE KEE FEELETOH

5. TA LEFTA TOOS EENAH KALA ALAH TA RR-RAFEEA
   TOOS EENAH SKOTEENA

The answers are:

1. HIS TOMATOES ARE DIRTY AND HIS BOSS WANTS
   PORK

2. HER COFFEE IS SWEET AND HER LAMB HAS CELERY

3. THEIR SISTERS ARE YOUNG BUT THEIR JOBS ARE
   DIRTY

4. HIS CAT IS SMALL BUT EATS VEAL AND FILLET
   STEAK

5. THEIR MONEY IS GOOD BUT THEIR OFFICES ARE
   DARK

Now cover up the answers below and translate the following:

(You can write your answers in)

1. HIS FATHER IS QUIET AND HIS LAMB IS SOFT
2. HER DOG IS BAD AND HER OFFICE IS DARK
3. HIS FIGS ARE BIG BUT HIS ICE CREAM HAS GARLIC
4. ITS GARDEN IS BEAUTIFUL AND ITS SHOP IS DRY
5. THEIR ROOMS ARE SMALL BUT THEIR LEMONADES ARE HERE

The answers are:

1. OH PATERAS TOO EENAH EESEEHOS KEH TOH ARNEE TOO EENAH MALAKOH

2. OH SKEELOS TEES EENAH KAKOS KEH TOH RAFEEOH TEES EENAH SKOTEENOH

3. TA SEEKAH TOO EENAH MERRALA ALAH TOH PAR-ROTOH TOO ECHEE SKORTHOH

4. OH KEEPOS TOO EENAH OREOS KEH TOH KATA-STEEMA TOO EENAH KSEROH

5. EE KAMARES TOOS EENAH MIKRES ALAH EE LEMON-ATHES TOOS EENAH ETHOH

198

SOME USEFUL QUESTION WORDS

THINK OF EACH IMAGE IN YOUR MIND'S EYE FOR ABOUT TEN SECONDS

○ The Greek for WHERE is POO
Imagine asking, "where is Winnie the POO?"

○ The Greek for WHY is YATEE
Imagine asking, "Why try to find the Himalayan YETI – the Abominable Snowman?"

○ The Greek for HOW is POS
Imagine asking, "How is this POSSible?"

○ The Greek for WHEN is PÓTE*
Imagine asking when you should put the baby on the POTTY.

○ The Greek for HOW MUCH is POSSO
Imagine asking, "How much is this PARCEL?"

*The accent on the "O" of PÓTE shows that this syllable is stressed; this is necessary because the stress on the second syllable, POTÉ, changes its meaning to NEVER.

YOU CAN WRITE YOUR ANSWERS IN

○ What is the English for POSSO? _____

○ What is the English for PÓTE? _____

○ What is the English for POS? _____

○ What is the English for YATEE? _____

○ What is the English for POO? _____

TURN BACK FOR THE ANSWERS

200

COVER UP THE LEFT HAND PAGE BEFORE ANSWERING

○ What is the Greek for how much? _____

○ What is the Greek for when? _____

○ What is the Greek for how? _____

○ What is the Greek for why? _____

○ What is the Greek for where? _____

TURN BACK FOR THE ANSWERS

ELEMENTARY GRAMMAR

You have just been given some question words.

To ask a question like WHERE IS THE HAT? you simply say POO EENAH TOH KAPELOH?

or to say

WHERE IS THE ROOM

you say

POO EENAH EE KAMARA?

Note that just as in English the verb comes right after the question word, and the noun follows.

For example,

WHERE ARE THE FIGS?	is	POO EENAH TA SEEKAH?
WHY ARE YOU HERE?	is	YATEE EESSEH ETHOH?
WHY IS MOTHER ANGRY	is	YATEE EENAH EE MEETERA THEEMOMENEE?
HOW ARE YOU?	is	POS EESSEH?
HOW DOES HE EAT THE MELON?	is	POS TROEE TOH PEPONEE?
WHEN IS SUNDAY?	is	POTE EENAH KEERYAKEE?
WHEN DOES SHE WANT THE MONEY?	is	POTE THELEE TA LEFTA?

Note that to say

HOW MUCH IS THE BEER?

you say

POSSO KANEE EE BEERA?

HOW MUCH IS THE SOUP? is POSSO KANEE EE SOOPA?

Also note that when you ask questions such as WHERE IS MY HAT?, it is asked in the form WHERE IS THE HAT MY?

In other words, words like MY, YOUR, OUR, etc., come at the end of the sentence.

So,

WHERE IS MY HAT is POO EENAH TOH KAPELOH MOO?

Now cover up the answers below and translate the following:

(You can write your answers in)

1. POO EENAH TOH PEREEPTEROH KEH POO EENAH TOH FARMAKEEOH?

2. YATEE THEN TROEE SKORTHOH ALAH TROEE MONOH FEELETOH?

3. POSSO KANEE TOH ARNEE KEH POO EENAH TOH HASAPEEKOH?

4. PÓTE THELEE TON MISTHO KEH YATEE VLEPEE TOH PLEENDEEREEOH?

5. POS EENAH OH PATERAS SOO KEH POSSO OREOH EENAH TOH PSOMEE?

The answers are:

1. WHERE IS THE KIOSK AND WHERE IS THE CHEMIST'S?

2. WHY DOESN'T HE (or SHE) EAT GARLIC BUT HE EATS ONLY FILLET STEAK?

3. HOW MUCH IS THE LAMB AND WHERE IS THE BUTCHER'S?

4. WHEN DOES HE (or SHE) WANT THE SALARY AND WHY DOES HE (or SHE) SEE THE LAUNDERETTE?

5. HOW IS YOUR FATHER AND HOW BEAUTIFUL IS THE BREAD?

Now cover up the answers below and translate the following:

(You can write your answers in)

1. WHERE IS THE WATER AND WHERE IS THE CREAM?

2. WHERE ARE MY GRAPES AND WHERE IS THE CHEQUE?

3. WHY IS THE CUCUMBER DIRTY AND THE HAIR- DRESSER'S OPEN?

4. WHEN DOES HE EAT MEAT, AND WHEN FISH?

5. HOW MUCH IS THE DRESS AND HOW MUCH IS THE ICE CREAM?

The answers are:

1. POO EENAH TOH NEROH KEH POO EENAH EE KREMA?

2. POO EENAH TA STAFEELYA MOO KEH POO EENAH EE EPEETAYEE?

3. YATEE EENAH TOH ANGOOREE VROMEEKOH KEH TOH KOMOTEEREEOH ANEECHTOH?

4. PÓTE TROEE KREAS, KEH PÓTE PSAREE?

5. POSSO KANEE TOH FOOSTANEE KEH POSSO KANEE TOH PARROTOH?

204

Section 8 TRAVELLING, THE CAR

THINK OF EACH IMAGE IN YOUR MIND'S EYE FOR ABOUT TEN SECONDS

○ The Greek for PASSPORT is THEEAVATEEREĘOH
  Imagine THEY HAVE A TEA ROOM where they issue
  passports.

○ The Greek for CUSTOMS is TELONEEOH
  Imagine looking at your knees and saying, "TELL OH KNEE
  OH, where are the customs?"

○ The Greek for SUITCASE is VALEETSA
  Imagine your VALET carrying a suitcase.

○ The Greek for TOILET is TOOALETA
  Imagine Greek gods meeting inside a toilet.

○ The Greek for TICKET is EESEETEEREEOH
  Imagine it is EASY TO RIO if you have an airline ticket.

○ The Greek for ENTRANCE is EESOTHOS (f)
  Imagine HE SAW US at the entrance.

○ The Greek for EXIT is EXOTHOS (f)
  Imagine the EXODUS was the exit from Egypt.

○ The Greek for DANGER is KEENTHEENOS
  Imagine shouting, "Danger, CLEAN THE NOSE."

○ The Greek for ARRIVAL is AFEEKSEE (f)
  Imagine someone saying, "I FIX EE up on your arrival in
  Greece."

○ The Greek for DEPARTURE is ANACHOREESEE (f)
  Imagine your departure ON A HORSY.

YOU CAN WRITE YOUR ANSWERS IN

○ What is the English for
ANACHOREESEE (f)?   _____

○ What is the English for AFEEKSEE (f)?   _____

○ What is the English for KEENTHEENOS?   _____

○ What is the English for EXOTHOS (f)?   _____

○ What is the English for EESOTHOS (f)?   _____

○ What is the English for
EESEETEEREEOH?   _____

○ What is the English for TOOALETA?   _____

○ What is the English for VALEETSA?   _____

○ What is the English for TELONEEOH?   _____

○ What is the English for
THEEAVATEEREEOH?   _____

TURN BACK FOR THE ANSWERS

COVER UP THE LEFT HAND PAGE BEFORE ANSWERING

○ What is the Greek for departure? _____

○ What is the Greek for arrival? _____

○ What is the Greek for danger? _____

○ What is the Greek for exit? _____

○ What is the Greek for entrance? _____

○ What is the Greek for ticket? _____

○ What is the Greek for toilet? _____

○ What is the Greek for suitcase? _____

○ What is the Greek for customs? _____

○ What is the Greek for passport? _____

TURN BACK FOR THE ANSWERS

SOME WORDS TO DO WITH CARS

THINK OF EACH IMAGE IN YOUR MIND'S EYE FOR ABOUT TEN SECONDS

○ The Greek for GARAGE is GARAZ
  Imagine Greek gods serving at a garage.

○ The Greek for PETROL is VENZEENEE
  Imagine BENZINE for sale as petrol.

○ The Greek for DIESEL OIL is PETRELEOH
  Imagine filling your car with diesel oil instead of PETROL.

○ The Greek for JACK is RREELOS*
  Imagine you REALISE you have forgotten your jack.

○ The Greek for IGNITION is MEEZA
  Imagine you always feel MISERable when you switch on the ignition.

○ The Greek for TANK is DEPOZITOH
  Imagine you DEPOSIT petrol in your tank.

○ The Greek for BONNET is KAPOH
  Imagine you leave your CAP ON the car bonnet.

○ The Greek for ENGINE is MEECHANEE (f)
  Imagine a MECHANICAL engine.

○ The Greek for BOOT is PORT BAGAZ
  Imagine you transPORT BAGGAGE in your boot.

*Remember that "RR" is a very soft sound at the back of the throat – like a "dirty" "G" sound.

YOU CAN WRITE YOUR ANSWERS IN

○ What is the English for PORT BAGAZ? _____

○ What is the English for MEECHANEE (f)? _____

○ What is the English for KAPOH? _____

○ What is the English for DEPOZITOH? _____

○ What is the English for MEEZA? _____

○ What is the English for RREELOS? _____

○ What is the English for PETRELEOH? _____

○ What is the English for VENZEENEE? _____

○ What is the English for GARAZ? _____

TURN BACK FOR THE ANSWERS

COVER UP THE LEFT HAND PAGE BEFORE ANSWERING

○ What is the Greek for boot? _____

○ What is the Greek for engine? _____

○ What is the Greek for bonnet? _____

○ What is the Greek for tank? _____

○ What is the Greek for ignition? _____

○ What is the Greek for jack? _____

○ What is the Greek for diesel oil? _____

○ What is the Greek for petrol? _____

○ What is the Greek for garage? _____

TURN BACK FOR THE ANSWERS

SOME MORE PERSONAL WORDS

THINK OF EACH IMAGE IN YOUR MIND'S EYE FOR ABOUT TEN SECONDS

The following words are only used for emphasis. Normally these words are not used, but they are given so that you will know what they are if you come across them.

○ The Greek for I is ERROH
  Imagine I am a HERO.

○ The Greek for YOU is ESEE
  Imagine you are EASY to please.

○ The Greek for HE is AFTOS
  Imagine he said, "HAVE TOAST."

○ The Greek for SHE is AFTEE
  Imagine she said, "HAVE TEA."

○ The Greek for IT is AFTOH
  Imagine it asked, "Do I HAVE TO?"

YOU CAN WRITE YOUR ANSWERS IN

○ What is the English for AFTOH?

○ What is the English for AFTEE?

○ What is the English for AFTOS?

○ What is the English for ERROH?

○ What is the English for ESEE?

TURN BACK FOR THE ANSWERS

COVER UP THE LEFT HAND PAGE BEFORE
ANSWERING

○ What is the Greek for it?

○ What is the Greek for she?

○ What is the Greek for he?

○ What is the Greek for I?

○ What is the Greek for you?

TURN BACK FOR THE ANSWERS

215

ELEMENTARY GRAMMAR

You may remember that THE MAN IS BIG is OH ANDRAS EENAH MERRALOS.

Now, <u>HE</u> IS BIG is AFTOS EENAH MERRALOS
and

 <u>HE</u> IS TALL   is AFTOS EENAH PSEELOS.

 <u>HE</u> IS MY HUSBAND is AFTOS EENAH OH ANDRAS
           MOO.

For FEMININE words, for example, <u>SHE</u> IS BEAUTIFUL, you simply say

 AFTEE EENAH OREA.

 SHE IS INSIDE THE ROOM is AFTEE EENAH MESA
          STEEN KAMARA.

 SHE EATS FISH   is AFTEE TROEE
          PSAREE

Finally, for NEUTER words, for example IT IS MY MELON, you say

 AFTOH EENAH TOH PEPONEE MOO.

 THIS IS YOUR PASSPORT is AFTOH EENAH TOH
          THEEAVATEEREOH
          SOO.

Note that you can use the words AFTOS, AFTEE and AFTOH equally when you want to say HE, SHE, IT or THIS.

So, for example,

 THIS WOMAN IS YOUNG is AFTEE EE
          YEENEKA EENAH
          NEA

 THIS SOUP IS GOOD   is AFTEE EE SOOPA
          EENAH KALEE

 THIS JACK IS OLD   is AFTOS OH RREELOS
          EENAH PALYOS

 THIS SALESMAN IS STUPID is AFTOS OH
          POLEETEES EENAH
          HAZOS

To say THIS DOG in Greek you say "this the dog", which is:

 AFTOS OH SKEELOS.

Also, THESE DOGS is AFTEE EE SKEELEE.

PLEASE NOTE: I, YOU, HE, SHE and IT are omitted unless you want to emphasise them.

Now cover up the answers below and translate the following:

(You can write your answers in)

1. POO EENAH AFTOH TOH FARMAKEEOH KEE AFTOH TOH TELONEEOH?

2. AFTEE EENAH EE VALEETSA MAS ALAH AFTOH THEN EENAH TOH HARTEE MAS

3. YATEE THELEE AFTOH TOH TEEREE KEE AFTOH TOH EESEETEEREEOH?

4. AFTOS OH KAFES EENAH RRLEEKOS ALAH AFTOH TOH GARAZ THEN ECHEE SKALA

5. AFTOS EENAH PEESOH APO TEEN PORTA ALAH AFTEE EENAH MESA STOH SKOTEENOH PEREEP-TEROH

The answers are:

1. WHERE IS THIS CHEMIST'S SHOP AND THIS CUSTOMS (OFFICE)?

2. THIS IS OUR SUITCASE BUT THIS IS NOT OUR PAPER

3. WHY DOES HE (or SHE) WANT THIS CHEESE AND THIS TICKET?

4. THIS COFFEE IS SWEET BUT THIS GARAGE DOESN'T HAVE (A) STAIRCASE

5. HE IS BEHIND THE DOOR BUT SHE IS INSIDE THE DARK KIOSK

217

Now cover up the answers below and translate the following:

(You can write your answers in)

1. THIS SHOP IS BIG AND THIS SUITCASE IS SMALL
2. SHE IS MY SISTER AND HE IS MY BROTHER
3. THIS BAKERY IS DIRTY BUT THIS ENGINE IS NOT QUIET
4. HE IS MY HUSBAND AND THIS EXIT IS DARK
5. IT IS HER DOG BUT THIS IS NOT HIS TANK

The answers are:

1. AFTOH TOH KATASTEEMA EENAH MERRALOH KEE AFTEE EE VALEETSA EENAH MIKREE
2. AFTEE EENAH EE ATHELFEE MOO KEE AFTOS EENAH OH ATHELFOS MOO
3. AFTOS OH FOORNOS EENAH VROMEEKOS ALAH AFTEE EE MEECHANEE THEN EENAH EESEEHEE
4. AFTOS EENAH OH ANDRAS MOO KEE AFTEE EE EXOTHOS EENAH SKOTEENEE
5. AFTOS EENAH OH SKEELOS TEES ALAH AFTOH THEN EENAH TOH DEPOZITOH TOO

MORE TRAVELLING WORDS

THINK OF EACH IMAGE IN YOUR MIND'S EYE FOR ABOUT TEN SECONDS

○ The Greek for TYRE is LASTICHO
Imagine you left your tyre in the LAST DITCH, OH!

○ The Greek for WHEEL is TROCHOS
Imagine TRUCKS with huge wheels.

○ The Greek for BRAKE is FRENOH
Imagine asking a FRIEND TO brake.

○ The Greek for STEERING WHEEL is TEEMONEE
Imagine spending all your TEA MONEY on a steering wheel.

○ The Greek for HORN is KLAXON
Imagine listening to a KLAXON horn.

○ The Greek for BOAT is PLEEOH
Imagine you get someone to PLAY OH so sweetly as you travel in a boat.

○ The Greek for CAR is AFTOKEENEETOH
Imagine you are AFTER KEEN HEATER prices for your car.

○ The Greek for COACH is PULLMAN
Imagine a PULLMAN coach.

○ The Greek for TRAIN is TRENOH
Imagine Greek gods boarding a train.

○ The Greek for AEROPLANE is AEROPLANOH
Imagine Greek gods throwing thunderbolts at your plane.

YOU CAN WRITE YOUR ANSWERS IN

○ What is the English for AEROPLANOH? _____

○ What is the English for TRENOH? _____

○ What is the English for PULLMAN? _____

○ What is the English for
AFTOKEENEETOH? _____

○ What is the English for PLEEOH? _____

○ What is the English for KLAXON? _____

○ What is the English for TEEMONEE? _____

○ What is the English for FRENOH? _____

○ What is the English for TROCHOS? _____

○ What is the English for LASTICHO? _____

TURN BACK FOR THE ANSWERS

COVER UP THE LEFT HAND PAGE BEFORE
ANSWERING

○ What is the Greek for aeroplane? _____

○ What is the Greek for train? _____

○ What is the Greek for coach? _____

○ What is the Greek for car? _____

○ What is the Greek for boat? _____

○ What is the Greek for horn? _____

○ What is the Greek for steering wheel? _____

○ What is the Greek for brake? _____

○ What is the Greek for wheel? _____

○ What is the Greek for tyre? _____

TURN BACK FOR THE ANSWERS

THE WORD "THEY"

THINK OF EACH IMAGE IN YOUR MIND'S EYE FOR ABOUT TEN SECONDS

○ The Greek for THEY [m] is AFTEE
  Imagine asking boys if THEY HAVE TEA too.

○ The Greek for THEY [f] is AFTES
  Imagine asking girls if THEY want AFTERS.

○ The Greek for THEY [n] is AFTAH
  Imagine looking at kittens AFTER THEY have been
  neutered.

Note: The above words are used for emphasis only.

YOU CAN WRITE YOUR ANSWERS IN

○ What is the English for AFTAH? _____

○ What is the English for AFTES? _____

○ What is the English for AFTEE? _____

TURN BACK FOR THE ANSWERS

COVER UP THE LEFT HAND PAGE BEFORE
ANSWERING

○ What is the Greek for they [n]? _____

○ What is the Greek for they [f]? _____

○ What is the Greek for they [m]? _____

TURN BACK FOR THE ANSWERS

ELEMENTARY GRAMMAR

You may remember that to say THE MEN ARE BIG you say EE ANDRES EENAH MERRALEE.

Now if you want to say THEY ARE BIG you simply say AFTEE EENAH MERRALEE, in the case of MASCULINE plural.

So, THEY ARE MY BROTHERS is AFTEE EENAH EE ATHELFEE MOO

You may note that AFTEE sounds quite like the feminine singular, but don't worry. You will be understood because the meaning also depends on the situation you are in.

For the FEMININE plural, to say THEY ARE MY SUITCASES you say AFTES EENAH EE VALEETSES MOO.

> THEY ARE HER SKIRTS   is AFTES EENAH EE FOOSTES TEES.

If you are using NEUTER words, then to say THEY ARE MY TICKETS you say AFTAH EENAH TA EESEETEEREEA MOO.

> THESE GRAPES ARE SWEET   is AFTAH TA STAFEELYA EENAH RRLEEKA.

Please note that you can also use the words AFTEE, AFTES and AFTAH when you want to say THESE.

> THESE SALARIES ARE GOOD   is AFTEE EE MISTHEE EENAH KALEE

> THESE MEN ARE TALL   is AFTEE EE ANDRES EENAH PSEELEE

> THESE TOMATOES ARE SMALL is AFTES EE DOMATES EENAH MIKRES

> THESE EGGS ARE NOT BIG   is AFTAH TA AVRRA THEN EENAH MERRALA

226

Now cover up the answers below and translate the following:

(You can write your answers in)

1. AFTES EE DOMATES EENAH MIKRES KEH AFTAH TA
   PLEEA EENAH KAFE

2. AFTEE EE ANDRES EENAH PSEELEE ALAH AFTEE EE
   TROCHEE EENAH MIKREE

3. AFTES EE KAMARES EENAH MERRALES KEH AFTAH
   TA LASTICHA EENAH ETHOH

4. AFTAH EENAH TA PAPOOTSYA MOO ALAH AFTAH TA
   TRENA EENAH EKEE

5. POO EENAH AFTAH TA AVRRA KEH YATEE AFTAH TA
   AFTOKEENEETA EENAH MAVRA?

The answers are:

1. THESE TOMATOES ARE SMALL AND THESE BOATS
   ARE BROWN

2. THESE MEN ARE TALL BUT THESE WHEELS ARE
   SMALL

3. THESE ROOMS ARE BIG AND THESE TYRES ARE HERE

4. THESE ARE MY SHOES BUT THESE TRAINS ARE
   THERE

5. WHERE ARE THESE EGGS AND WHY ARE THESE
   CARS BLACK?

Now cover up the answers below and translate the following:

(You can write your answers in)

1. THEY ARE BEAUTIFUL (referring to women)
2. THESE ARE MY SISTERS
3. THESE BEANS ARE BAD
4. WHERE ARE THEY? (referring to men)
5. THEY ARE MY FATHER AND MY BROTHER
6. THEY ARE NOT OUR BRAKES
7. THESE DANGERS ARE BIG
8. THESE CARS ARE BEHIND THESE TRAINS
9. THESE JACKS ARE INSIDE YOUR BONNET/HOOD
10. THESE IGNITIONS ARE NOT GOOD

The answers are:

1. AFTES EENAH OREES
2. AFTES EENAH EE ATHELFES MOO
3. AFTAH TA FASOLYA EENAH KAKA
4. POU EENAH AFTEE?
5. AFTEE EENAH OH PATERAS MOO KEE OH ATHELFOS MOO
6. AFTAH THEN EENAH TA FRENA MAS
7. AFTEE EE KEENTHEENEE EENAH MERRALEE
8. AFTAH TA AFTOKEENEETA EENAH PEESOH APOH AFTAH TA TRENA
9. AFTEE EE RREELEE EENAH MESA STOH KAPOH SOO
10. AFTES EE MEEZES THEN EENAH KALES

228

Section 9 LEISURE ACTIVITY

THINK OF EACH IMAGE IN YOUR MIND'S EYE FOR ABOUT TEN SECONDS

○ The Greek for BEACH is AMOOTHYA
Imagine when I see a beach I MOVE THERE.

○ The Greek for SAND is AMOS (f)
Imagine A MOSque surrounded by sand.

○ The Greek for TOWEL is PETSETA
Imagine your BED SITTER covered in towels.

○ The Greek for PICNIC is PICNIC (n)
Imagine Greek gods at a picnic.

○ The Greek for SUN is EELYOS
Imagine thinking perhaps the sun can HEAL US.

○ The Greek for COLD is KREEOH
Imagine it is cold in KOREA.

○ The Greek for SEA is THALASSA
Imagine THE LASER was first used in the sea.

○ The Greek for HEAT is ZESTEE (f)
Imagine you look forward to the heat with great ZEST.

○ The Greek for TIDE is PALEERYA
Imagine your PALS HEAR YOU when the tide comes in.

○ The Greek for WAVE is KEEMA (n)
Imagine saying, "Give me your KEY MA! A wave is going to get you."

YOU CAN WRITE YOUR ANSWERS IN

○ What is the English for KEEMA (n)? _____

○ What is the English for PALEERYA? _____

○ What is the English for ZESTEE (f)? _____

○ What is the English for THALASSA? _____

○ What is the English for KREEOH? _____

○ What is the English for EELYOS? _____

○ What is the English for PICNIC (n)? _____

○ What is the English for PETSETA? _____

○ What is the English for AMOS (f)? _____

○ What is the English for AMOOTHYA? _____

TURN BACK FOR THE ANSWERS

COVER UP THE LEFT HAND PAGE BEFORE
ANSWERING

○ What is the Greek for wave? _____

○ What is the Greek for tide? _____

○ What is the Greek for heat? _____

○ What is the Greek for sea? _____

○ What is the Greek for cold? _____

○ What is the Greek for sun? _____

○ What is the Greek for picnic? _____

○ What is the Greek for towel? _____

○ What is the Greek for sand? _____

○ What is the Greek for beach? _____*

TURN BACK FOR THE ANSWERS

*Another word for BEACH is PARALIA

ELEMENTARY GRAMMAR

You may remember that to say THE MAN WANTS, you say OH ANDRAS THELEE.

Now, if you want to say I WANT, you say THELO.
That is, you change the -EE ending to -O.
  For example,

I WANT THE GLASS	is THELO TOH POTEEREE
I HAVE THE TICKET	is ECHO TOH EESEETEEREEOH
I HAVE THE SUITCASE	is ECHO TEEN VALEETSA
I SEE THE BEACH	is VLEPO TEEN AMOOTHYA
I EAT GARLIC	is TROO SKORTHOH
I DON'T SEE THE SEA	is THEN VLEPO TEEN THALASSA

To say "YOU WANT" when talking to one person, you say THELEES.

In other words, the verb ends with "EES".

Now cover up the answers below and translate the following:

(You can write your answers in)

1. VLEPO TEEN THALASSA ALAH THEN VLEPO TEEN AMOOTHYA

2. THEN THELO TOH KRASEE ALAH THELO TEEN PETSETA

3. ECHO TAH LEFTA ALAH OH EELYOS THEN EENAH ETHOH

4. THEN TROO PSOMEE KEH TOH KEEMA EENAH MERRALOH

5. THEN VLEPO TOH PLEEOH ALAH THEN TROO TEEN AMO

The answers are:

1. I SEE THE SEA BUT I DON'T SEE THE BEACH

2. I DON'T WANT THE WINE BUT I WANT THE TOWEL

3. I HAVE THE MONEY BUT THE SUN IS NOT HERE

4. I DON'T EAT BREAD AND THE WAVE IS BIG

5. I DON'T SEE THE BOAT BUT I DON'T EAT THE SAND

Now cover up the answers below and translate the following:

(You can write your answers in)

1. I SEE THE BEACH BUT I DON'T WANT THE PICNIC
2. I DON'T HAVE THE VEAL BUT I HAVE THE STEERING WHEEL
3. I DON'T WANT THE CAKE AND I WANT THE HORN
4. I EAT LAMB BUT I DON'T EAT PETROL
5. I DON'T EAT MEAT AND EGGS AND I SEE THE ENTRANCE

The answers are:

1. VLEPO TEEN AMOOTHYA ALAH THEN THELO TOH PICNIC
2. THEN ECHO TOH MOSCHAREE ALAH ECHO TOH TEEMONEE
3. THEN THELO TOH RRLEEKO KEH THELO TOH KLAXON
4. TROO ARNEE ALAH THEN TROO VENZEENEE
5. THEN TROO KREAS KEE AVRRA KEE VLEPO TEEN EESOTHO

SCENERY

THINK OF EACH IMAGE IN YOUR MIND'S EYE FOR ABOUT TEN SECONDS

○ The Greek for RIVER is POTAMEE
  Imagine you have to swim in rivers if you study BOTANY.

○ The Greek for LAKE is LIMNEE (f)
  Imagine they found a LIMB NEar a lake.

○ The Greek for FOREST is THASSOS (n)
  Imagine they poured THE SAUCE over the forest.

○ The Greek for MOUNTAIN is VOONOH
  Imagine saying, "Look at the VIEW NOW from the mountain."

○ The Greek for CASTLE is CASTROH
  Imagine Fidel CASTRO of Cuba looking out from a castle.

○ The Greek for CHURCH is EKLEESYA
  Imagine ECCLESIASTICAL meetings in a church.

○ The Greek for TEMPLE is NAOS
  Imagine sticking your NOSE inside a temple.

○ The Greek for PALACE is PALATEE
  Imagine Greek gods dining at a palace.

○ The Greek for ANCIENT SITES is ARCHEA (n plural)
  Imagine all the best ancient sites ARE HERE in Greece.

○ The Greek for MUSEUM is MOOSSEEOH
  Imagine a museum full of statues of Greek gods.

YOU CAN WRITE YOUR ANSWERS IN

○ What is the English for MOOSSEEOH? _____

○ What is the English for ARCHEA (n plural)? _____

○ What is the English for PALATEE? _____

○ What is the English for NAOS? _____

○ What is the English for EKLEESYA? _____

○ What is the English for CASTROH? _____

○ What is the English for VOONOH? _____

○ What is the English for THASSOS (n)? _____

○ What is the English for LIMNEE (f)? _____

○ What is the English for POTAMEE? _____

TURN BACK FOR THE ANSWERS

COVER UP THE LEFT HAND PAGE BEFORE ANSWERING

○ What is the Greek for museum? _____

○ What is the Greek for ancient sites? _____

○ What is the Greek for palace? _____

○ What is the Greek for temple? _____

○ What is the Greek for church? _____

○ What is the Greek for castle? _____

○ What is the Greek for mountain? _____

○ What is the Greek for forest? _____

○ What is the Greek for lake? _____

○ What is the Greek for river? _____

TURN BACK FOR THE ANSWERS

ELEMENTARY GRAMMAR

Now, if you want to say YOU EAT BREAD when you are talking to many people, you simply say TROTE PSOMEE.

That is, you add the ending -TE to the verb.
For example,

YOU EAT FISH	is TROTE PSAREE
YOU SEE THE DOG	is VLEPETE TON SKEELO
YOU DON'T SEE THE CAT	is THEN VLEPETE TEEN RRATA
YOU WANT THE TICKET	is THELETE TOH EESEETEEREEOH
DO YOU WANT THE WINE?	is THELETE TOH KRASEE?
YOU HAVE MONEY	is ECHETE LEFTA
YOU DON'T HAVE THE CAR	is THEN ECHETE TOH AFTOKEENEETOH

Now cover up the answers below and translate the following:

(You can write your answers in)

1. VLEPETE TOH VOONOH? THEN VLEPETE TOH MOOSSEEOH?

2. THEN VLEPETE TON EELYO ALAH VLEPETE TEEN EKLEESYA

3. ECHETE TEEN PETSETA ALAH THEN ECHETE TOH PALATEE

4. THELETE TOH LATHEE ALAH THEN THELETE TOH POTAMEE

5. TROTE TOH KREAS ALAH THEN ECHETE TON NAO

The answers are:

1. DO YOU SEE THE MOUNTAIN? DON'T YOU SEE THE MUSEUM?

2. YOU DON'T SEE THE SUN BUT YOU SEE THE CHURCH

3. YOU HAVE THE TOWEL BUT YOU DON'T HAVE THE PALACE

4. YOU WANT THE OIL BUT YOU DON'T WANT THE RIVER

5. YOU EAT THE MEAT BUT YOU DON'T HAVE THE TEMPLE

Now cover up the answers below and translate the following:

(You can write your answers in)

Note: In the following examples translate you as plural.

1. YOU EAT ONION AND GARLIC BUT YOU DON'T EAT
   FIGS

2. YOU DON'T SEE THE BOAT BUT YOU SEE THE CASTLE
   ON THE MOUNTAIN

3. YOU DON'T HAVE THE TICKET BUT YOU ALWAYS
   HAVE THE PASSPORT

4. DO YOU WANT THE WATER? DON'T YOU WANT THE
   OLIVE?

5. YOU WANT THE TOWEL BUT YOU DON'T WANT THE
   ANCIENT SITES

The answers are:

1. TROTE KREMEETHEE KEH SKORTHOH ALAH THEN
   TROTE SEEKA

2. THEN VLEPETE TOH PLEEOH ALAH VLEPETE TOH
   CASTROH PANOH STOH VOONOH

3. THEN ECHETE TOH EESEETEEREEOH ALAH ECHETE
   PANDA TOH THEEAVATEEREEOH

4. THELETE TOH NEROH? THEN THELETE TEEN ELYA?

5. THELETE TEEN PETSETA ALAH THEN THELETE TA
   ARCHEA

SOME USEFUL WORDS

THINK OF EACH IMAGE IN YOUR MIND'S EYE FOR ABOUT TEN SECONDS

○ The Greek for DOCTOR is YATROS
  Imagine YOU TRUST a doctor.

○ The Greek for POLICE is ASTINOMEEA
  Imagine the police are AS THIN AS ME, AH!

○ The Greek for BANK is TRAPEZA
  Imagine a TRAP IS A bank. They take your money.

○ The Greek for CAMP SITE is CAMPING
  Imagine CAMPING at a camp site.

○ The Greek for TIN CAN is KONSERVA
  Imagine you CONSERVE food in tin cans.

○ The Greek for TENT is SKINEE (f)
  Imagine a SKINNY man getting into a tent.

○ The Greek for LETTER is RR-RAMA (n)
  Imagine a DRAMA over posting a letter.

○ The Greek for POSTCARD is KARTA
  Imagine ex-President Jimmy CARTER reading a postcard.

○ The Greek for STREET is OTHOS (f)
  Imagine OTHERS live in your street.

○ The Greek for MAP is HARTEES
  Imagine your HEART IS where your map is.

YOU CAN WRITE YOUR ANSWERS IN

○ What is the English for HARTEES? _____

○ What is the English for OTHOS (f)? _____

○ What is the English for KARTA? _____

○ What is the English for RR-RAMA (n)? _____

○ What is the English for SKINEE (f)? _____

○ What is the English for KONSERVA? _____

○ What is the English for CAMPING? _____

○ What is the English for TRAPEZA? _____

○ What is the English for ASTINOMEEA? _____

○ What is the English for YATROS? _____

TURN BACK FOR THE ANSWERS

242

COVER UP THE LEFT HAND PAGE BEFORE ANSWERING

○ What is the Greek for map? _____

○ What is the Greek for street? _____

○ What is the Greek for postcard? _____

○ What is the Greek for letter? _____

○ What is the Greek for tent? _____

○ What is the Greek for tin can? _____

○ What is the Greek for camp site? _____

○ What is the Greek for bank? _____

○ What is the Greek for police? _____

○ What is the Greek for doctor? _____

TURN BACK FOR THE ANSWERS

ELEMENTARY GRAMMAR

When you want to say   THE DOG AND THE CAT WANT
         you say   OH SKEELOS KEE EE RRATA
                  THELOON.

That is, you add the ending -OON to the verb.

For example,

THE BIG FISH WANT THE SMALL . . .	is TA MERRALA PSARYA THELOON TA MIKRA
THE BOYS DON'T SEE THE GIRLS	is TA ARROHRYA THEN VLE-POON TA KOREETSYA
DO THEY WANT THE SUGAR?	is AFTEE THELOON TEEN ZAHAREE?
THEY DON'T SEE THE WAVE	is AFTEE THEN VLEPOON TOH KEEMA
THEY HAVE THE ROOM	is AFTEE ECHOON TEEN KAMARA
DO THEY HAVE MONEY?	is AFTEE ECHOON LEFTA?

Note that the verb EAT is a small exception to this rule. It makes the plural with the ending -ON instead of -OON.

For example,

DO THEY EAT BREAD?	is AFTEE TRON PSOMEE?
THE CATS EAT FISH	is EE RRATES TRON PSAREE
WHY DO THEY EAT MEAT?	is YATEE AFTEE TRON KREAS?
THEY DON'T EAT RICE	is AFTEE (AFTES) THEN TRON REEZEE

244

Now cover up the answers below and translate the following:

(You can write your answers in)

1. TA AFTOKEENEETA THEN ECHOON VENZEENEE KEE EE TRAPEZES THEN ECHOON LEFTA

2. AFTES THEN VLEPOON TOH POTAMEE ALAH VLEPOON TEEN KOKEENEE AMOOTHYA

3. AFTEE THEN THELOON TON EELYO ALAH THELOON TEEN PALEERYA

4. POTE AFTEE TRON RRLEEKA KEH POTE THEN TRON MOSCHAREE?

5. TA AFENDEEKA THEN TRON ELYES ALAH TA SOSTA EESEETEEREEA ECHOON ARITHMO

The answers are:

1. THE CARS DON'T HAVE PETROL AND THE BANKS DON'T HAVE MONEY

2. THEY DON'T SEE THE RIVER BUT (THEY) SEE THE RED BEACH

3. THEY DON'T WANT THE SUN BUT (THEY) WANT THE TIDE

4. WHEN DO THEY EAT CAKES (SWEETS) AND WHEN DON'T THEY EAT VEAL?

5. THE BOSSES DON'T EAT OLIVES BUT THE CORRECT TICKETS HAVE (A) NUMBER

Now cover up the answers below and translate the following:

(You can write your answers in)

1. THEY (f) WANT THE TENT BUT THEY DON'T WANT THE POLICE

2. THE DOGS DON'T EAT THE TIN CAN AND THE GIRLS SEE THE DOCTOR

3. DO THEY (m) SEE THE TEMPLE? BUT THEY DON'T SEE THE LETTER

4. THE MEN DON'T HAVE JOBS BUT THEY WANT THE BANK

5. WHY DON'T THEY (m) EAT LAMB? BUT THEY EAT OUR POSTCARD

The answers are:

1. AFTES THELOON TEEN SKINEE ALAH THEN THELOON TEEN ASTINOMEEA

2. EE SKEELEE THEN TRON TEEN KONSERVA KEH TA KOREETSYA VLEPOON TON YATRO

3. AFTEE VLEPOON TON NAO? ALAH THEN VLEPOON TOH RR-RAMA

4. EE ANDRES THEN ECHOON THOOLYES ALAH AFTEE THELOON TEEN TRAPEZA

5. YATEE THEN TRON ARNEE? ALAH TRON TEEN KARTA MAS

Section 10 AT THE DOCTOR'S, EMERGENCY WORDS, USEFUL WORDS

THINK OF EACH IMAGE IN YOUR MIND'S EYE FOR ABOUT TEN SECONDS

○ The Greek for PAIN is PONOS
Imagine a terrible pain is UPON US.

○ The Greek for ILLNESS is AROSTYA
Imagine a doctor says, "I ROAST YOU to get rid of your illness."

○ The Greek for COUGH is VEECHAS (m)
Imagine a VICIOUS cough.

○ The Greek for TOOTH is THONDEE
Imagine you have a sore tooth every SUNDAY.

○ The Greek for FACE is PROSOPOH
Imagine you have a PROSPEROUS looking face.

○ The Greek for EYE is MATEE
Imagine MY TEA is in your eye.

○ The Greek for NOSE is MEETEE (f)
Imagine punching your nose and making it MEATY.

○ The Greek for ARM is BRATSOH
Imagine you hit a BRAT SO hard, you broke his arm.

○ The Greek for HAND is HEAIREE
Imagine a HAIRY hand.

○ The Greek for LEG is POTHEE
Imagine watching a dog PAW THE leg of another dog.

YOU CAN WRITE YOUR ANSWERS IN

○ What is the English for POTHEE? _____

○ What is the English for HEAIREE? _____

○ What is the English for BRATSOH? _____

○ What is the English for MEETEE (f)? _____

○ What is the English for MATEE? _____

○ What is the English for PROSOPOH? _____

○ What is the English for THONDEE? _____

○ What is the English for VEECHAS (m)? _____

○ What is the English for AROSTYA? _____

○ What is the English for PONOS? _____

TURN BACK FOR THE ANSWERS

COVER UP THE LEFT HAND PAGE BEFORE
ANSWERING

○ What is the Greek for leg?   _____

○ What is the Greek for hand?   _____

○ What is the Greek for arm?   _____

○ What is the Greek for nose?   _____

○ What is the Greek for eye?   _____

○ What is the Greek for face?   _____

○ What is the Greek for tooth?   _____

○ What is the Greek for cough?   _____

○ What is the Greek for illness?   _____

○ What is the Greek for pain?   _____

TURN BACK FOR THE ANSWERS

ELEMENTARY GRAMMAR

You may remember that in sentences such as THE DOG SEES THE CAT, the cat is the object of the sentence.

In Greek the word for THE then becomes TON, TEEN or TOH – according to whether the object of the sentence is masculine, feminine or neuter.

For example,

THE DOG EATS THE BATHING SUIT is	OH SKEELOS TROEE TOH MAYOH
THE FATHER SEES THE CHAIR is	OH PATERAS VLEPEE TEEN KAREKLA
THE GIRL HAS THE LOBSTER is	TOH KOREETSEE ECHEE TON ASTAKO

Now, in sentences such as THE GIRLS EAT THE LOBSTERS, the object of the sentence (the lobsters) is in the plural.

So, in Greek you say TA KOREETSYA TRON TOOS ASTAKOOS.

In other words, if the object of the sentence is masculine and plural, the word for THE becomes TOOS, and the ending of the word itself changes from -OS to -OOS.

For example,

THE MEN SEE THE DOGS is EE ANDRES VLEPOON TOOS SKEELOS

Now, if you want to say THE WOMEN WANT THE CHAIRS, since the word CHAIR is KAREKLA, 'chairs' is feminine and plural. So you say: EE YEENEKES THELOON TEES KAREKLES.

In other words, if the object of the sentence is feminine and plural, the word for THE becomes TEES and the ending of the word itself changes from -A to -ES.

For example,

> THE FATHER WANTS THE TOMATOES   is   OH PATERAS THELEE TEES DOMATES
>
> I HAVE THE CHEQUES   is   ECHO TEES EPEETAYES

Finally, if you want to say I HAVE THE SHOES, you simply say ECHO TA PAPOOTSYA.

In other words if the object of the sentence is neuter and plural the word for THE is TA and the ending of the word itself remains -A – like in all neuter plurals.

For example,

> THEY WANT THE KNIVES   is   AFTEE THELOON TA MACHERYA
>
> THE GIRLS EAT THE BIRDS   is   TA KOREETSYA TRON TA POOLYA

Do not worry if you make mistakes. Provided you get the basic vocabulary correct you will almost always be understood.

Now cover up the answers below and translate the following:

(You can write your answers in)

1. THEN ECHETE TA PRASEENA KAPELA ALAH ECHETE TA HAZA ZAWA

2. AFTOS VLEPEE TOOS SKEELOOS ALAH THEN THELEE TEES PETSETES

3. AFTEE TROEE TEES PATATES MAS KEE AFTEE THELEE EPEESEES TA STAFEELYA MAS

4. THEN THELO TA MERRALA POTEERYA ALAH THELO TA ASPRA TEERYA

5. THEN TROTE TEES OREES DOMATES ALAH ECHETE TEES SOSTES AROSTYES

The answers are:

1. YOU DON'T HAVE THE GREEN HATS BUT YOU HAVE THE STUPID ANIMALS

2. HE SEES THE DOGS BUT HE DOESN'T WANT THE TOWELS

3. SHE EATS OUR POTATOES AND SHE ALSO WANTS OUR GRAPES

4. I DON'T WANT THE BIG GLASSES BUT I WANT THE WHITE CHEESE(S)

5. YOU DON'T EAT THE BEAUTIFUL TOMATOES BUT YOU HAVE THE CORRECT ILLNESSES

Now cover up the answers below and translate the following:

(You can write your answers in)

1. THE GIRLS WANT THE BLUE SKIRTS AND THE WHITE TEETH

2. THE BANK HAS THE OLD CHEQUES AND THE FACE HAS (THE) TWO EYES

3. YOU SEE THE BIG TEMPLES BUT YOU DON'T SEE OUR LEGS

4. I EAT THE GREEN LETTUCES AND I HAVE THE BIG HAND

5. HE WANTS THE SMALL LOBSTERS AND THE COLD DAYS

The answers are:

1. TA KOREETSYA THELOON TEES BLE FOOSTES KEH TA ASPRA THONDYA

2. EE TRAPEZA ECHEE TEES PALYES EPEETAYES KEH TOH PROSOPOH ECHEE (TA) THEEOH MATYA

3. VLEPETE TOOS MERRALOOS NAOOS ALAH THEN VLEPETE TA POTHYA MAS

4. TROO TA PRASEENA MAROOLYA KEE ECHO TA MER-RALA HEAIREE

5. AFTOS THELEE TOOS MIKROS ASTAKOOS KEH TEES KREE-ES MERES

EMERGENCY WORDS

THINK OF EACH IMAGE IN YOUR MIND'S EYE FOR ABOUT TEN SECONDS

○ The Greek for HOSPITAL is NOSSOKOMEEOH
Imagine an Italian saying, "NO SOCK ME OH! or I end up in hospital."

○ The Greek for PLASTER is HANZAPLAST*
Imagine covering your HANDS IN PLASTer.

○ The Greek for AMBULANCE is ASTHENOFOROH
Imagine if you are injured ASK THEN FOR AN ambulance.

○ The Greek for ACCIDENT is THISTICHEEMA (n)
Imagine THIS STIGMA will stay with you after an accident.

○ The Greek for THIEF is KLEFTEES (m)
Imagine a thief LEFT HIS fingerprints.

○ The Greek for FIRE is FOTYA
Imagine you PHOTO A fire.

○ The Greek for TELEPHONE is TEELEFONO
Imagine Greek gods telephoning each other.

○ The Greek for BLOOD is EMAH (n)
Imagine EMMA, Lord Nelson's friend, covered in blood.

○ The Greek for HELP! is VOYEETHEEA!
Imagine you hear a VOICE HERE shouting "HELP!"

○ The Greek for STING is TSEEMBEEMA (n)
Imagine you were SEEN BY MY doctor for a bee sting.

* Sticking plaster.

255

YOU CAN WRITE YOUR ANSWERS IN

○ What is the English for TSEEMBEEMA (n)? _____

○ What is the English for VOYEETHEEA!? _____

○ What is the English for EMAH (n)? _____

○ What is the English for TEELEFONO? _____

○ What is the English for FOTYA? _____

○ What is the English for KLEFTEES (m)? _____

○ What is the English for THISTICHEEMA (n)? _____

○ What is the English for ASTHENOFO-ROH? _____

○ What is the English for HANZAPLAST? _____

○ What is the English for NOSSOKOMEE-OH? _____

TURN BACK FOR THE ANSWERS

COVER UP THE LEFT HAND PAGE BEFORE ANSWERING

○ What is the Greek for sting? _____

○ What is the Greek for help!? _____

○ What is the Greek for blood? _____

○ What is the Greek for telephone? _____

○ What is the Greek for fire? _____

○ What is the Greek for thief? _____

○ What is the Greek for accident? _____

○ What is the Greek for ambulance? _____

○ What is the Greek for plaster? _____

○ What is the Greek for hospital? _____

TURN BACK FOR THE ANSWERS

VERBS

THINK OF EACH IMAGE IN YOUR MIND'S EYE FOR ABOUT TEN SECONDS

○ The Greek for I DRINK is PEENO
  Imagine PINOCCIO, the puppet, drinking something.

○ The Greek for I RUN is TRECHO
  Imagine I run through TREACLE.

○ The Greek for I MAKE is KANO
  Imagine you make a CANOE.
  N.B. Kano also means DO.

○ The Greek for I SPEAK is MEELÓ
  Imagine you make a MEAL O' speaking Greek.

YOU CAN WRITE YOUR ANSWERS IN

○ What is the English for MEELÓ? _____

○ What is the English for KANO? _____

○ What is the English for TRECHO? _____

○ What is the English for PEENO? _____

TURN BACK FOR THE ANSWERS

COVER UP THE LEFT HAND PAGE BEFORE ANSWERING

○ What is the Greek for I speak?　　　　_____

○ What is the Greek for I make?　　　　_____

○ What is the Greek for I run?　　　　　_____

○ What is the Greek for I drink?　　　　_____

TURN BACK FOR THE ANSWERS

ELEMENTARY GRAMMAR

You have just learned four verbs:

PEENO	I DRINK
TRECHO	I RUN
KANO	I MAKE/DO
MEELÓ	I SPEAK

You may remember that if you want to say I WANT in Greek, you say THELO. If you want to say HE WANTS you simply say AFTOS THELEE.

The same endings apply to the four new verbs.

For example,

SHE DRINKS WATER	is AFTEE PEENEE NEROH
I MAKE THE CAKE	is KANO TOH RRLEEKOH
I DON'T SPEAK	is THEN MEELO
I DON'T RUN MUCH	is THEN TRECHO POLEE
HE MAKES THE SALAD	is AFTOS KANEE TEEN SALATA
THE DOG RUNS IN THE ROOM	is OH SKEELOS TRECHEE MESA STEEN KAMARA
THE SMALL GIRL DOESN'T SPEAK	is TOH MIKROH KOREETSEE THEN MEELEE

Please note: in Greek you say KANEE ZESTEE or KANEE KREEOH in order to say IT IS HOT or IT IS COLD.

In other words, you say IT MAKES COLD or IT MAKES HEAT.

Now cover up the answers below and translate the following:

(You can write your answers in)

1. POTE AFTOS PEENEE TSAEE?
2. TOH KOREETSEE TRECHEE MESA STON KEEPO
3. AFTOS MEELEE PANDA TELEFTEOS
4. THEN KANO OREOH KRASEE
5. EE MEETERA KANEE TEEN SALATA

The answers are:

1. WHEN DOES HE DRINK TEA?
2. THE GIRL RUNS IN THE GARDEN
3. HE ALWAYS SPEAKS LAST
4. I DON'T MAKE BEAUTIFUL WINE
5. THE MOTHER MAKES THE SALAD

Now cover up the answers below and translate the following:

(You can write your answers in)

1. SEEMERA KANEE KREEOH, ALAH TOH MESSEE-MEREE KANEE ZESTEE

2. AFTEE PEENEE PANDA KRASEE KEE AFTOS THEN PEENEE POTEH NEROH

3. TOH GARSONEE THEN MEELEE MESA STOH RESTORAN

4. TOH AEROPLANOH TRECHEE PEEOH POLEE APOH TOH AFTOKEENEETOH

5. OH POLEETEES THEN KANEE TON SOSTOH KAFE

The answers are:

1. TODAY IT IS COLD, BUT AT MIDDAY IT IS HOT

2. SHE ALWAYS DRINKS WINE AND HE NEVER DRINKS WATER

3. THE WAITER DOESN'T SPEAK INSIDE THE RESTAURANT

4. THE AEROPLANE RUNS MORE THAN THE CAR

5. THE SALESMAN DOESN'T MAKE THE CORRECT COFFEE

Now cover up the answers below and translate the following:

(You can write your answers in)

1. I DRINK WATER BUT I DON'T DRINK WINE
2. THE CAT RUNS AFTER THE DOG
3. THE MOTHER MAKES THE SOUP AND THE SALAD
4. HE NEVER SPEAKS INSIDE THE HOSPITAL
5. WHY DON'T I DO THIS JOB?
6. SHE DOESN'T SPEAK AFTER THE ACCIDENT
7. THE BLOOD RUNS FROM MY NOSE
8. THE THIEF NEVER DRINKS WINE
9. THE BANK MAKES MONEY
10. I DON'T SPEAK INSIDE THE CHURCH

The answers are:

1. PEENO NEROH ALAH THEN PEENO KRASEE
2. EE RRATA TRECHEE META APOH TON SKEELO
3. EE MEETERA KANEE TEEN SOOPA KEH TEEN SALATA
4. (AFTOS) THEN MEELEE POTEH MESA STOH NOSOKOMEEOH
5. YATEE THEN KANO AFTEE TEEN THOOYA?
6. (AFTEE) THEN MEELEE META APOH TOH THIS-TICHEEMA
7. TOH EMAH TRECHEE APOH TEEN MEETEE MOO
8. OH KLEFTEES THEN PEENEE POTEH KRASEE
9. EE TRAPEZA KANEE LEFTA
10. THEN MEELO MESA STEEN EKLEESYA

THE BODY

THINK OF EACH IMAGE IN YOUR MIND'S EYE FOR ABOUT TEN SECONDS

○ The Greek for MOUTH is STOMA (n)
   Imagine your mouth leads to your STOMAch.

○ The Greek for NECK is LEMOS
   Imagine LEMONS growing out of your neck.

○ The Greek for EAR is AFTEE
   Imagine you HAVE TO have ears.

○ The Greek for STOMACH is STOMACHEE
   Imagine Greek gods admiring their stomachs.

○ The Greek for HEART is KARTHYA
   Imagine CARDIAC problems are heart problems.

○ The Greek for BOIL is SPEEREE
   Imagine a doctor SPEARING a boil.

○ The Greek for FLU is RR-REEPEE (f)
   Imagine being WEEPY because you have flu – but remember the word is RREEPEE.*

○ The Greek for DIARRHOEA is THE ARIA
   Imagine Maria Calas singing THE ARIA from *Don Giovanni*, while suffering from diarrhoea.

○ The Greek for PILL is HAPEE
   Imagine being HAPPY to swallow a pill.

○ The Greek for MEDICINE is FARMAKOH
   Imagine getting medicine from a PHARMACY.

*Remember a "rr" in this course is pronounced very softly at the back of the throat – like a very rough "g".

YOU CAN WRITE YOUR ANSWERS IN

○ What is the English for FARMAKOH? _____

○ What is the English for HAPEE? _____

○ What is the English for THE ARIA? _____

○ What is the English for RR-REEPEE (f)? _____

○ What is the English for SPEEREE? _____

○ What is the English for KARTHYA? _____

○ What is the English for STOMACHEE? _____

○ What is the English for AFTEE? _____

○ What is the English for LEMOS? _____

○ What is the English for STOMA (n)? _____

TURN BACK FOR THE ANSWERS

COVER UP THE LEFT HAND PAGE BEFORE
ANSWERING

○ What is the Greek for medicine? _____

○ What is the Greek for pill? _____

○ What is the Greek for diarrhoea? _____

○ What is the Greek for flu? _____

○ What is the Greek for boil? _____

○ What is the Greek for heart? _____

○ What is the Greek for stomach? _____

○ What is the Greek for ear? _____

○ What is the Greek for neck? _____

○ What is the Greek for mouth? _____

TURN BACK FOR THE ANSWERS

ELEMENTARY GRAMMAR

You may remember that if you want to say YOU SEE, when talking to many people, you say VLEPETE. That is, you add the ending -TE to the verb.

Similarly, if you want to say THEY SEE, you say VLEPOON. That is, you add the ending -OON to the verb.

The same rules apply to the verbs you have just learned.

So,

YOU DRINK WINE	is PEENETE KRASEE
YOU MAKE CAKES	is KANETE RRLEEKA
YOU SPEAK MUCH	is MEELATE POLEE
YOU ALWAYS RUN	is TRECHETE PANDA
THEY DON'T DRINK BEER	is AFTES (AFTEE) THEN PEENOON BEERA
THEY MAKE MONEY	is AFTES (AFTEE) KANOON LEFTA
THE CATS DON'T SPEAK	is EE RRATES THEN MEELOON
THE DOGS DON'T RUN	is EE SKEELEE THEN TRECHOON

Now cover up the answers below and translate the following:

(You can write your answers in)

1. EE RRATES PEENOON NEROH KEE RRALA ALAH EE
   KLEFTES PEENOON KAFE

2. TA KOREETSYA TRECHOON KATOH APOH TEES
   SKALES KEE PANOH STA TRAPEZYA

3. EE YEENEKES KANOON OREES SOOPES ALAH THEN
   KANOON KALEE BEERA

4. EE ANDRES THEN MEELOON PREEN APOH TEES
   YEENEKES ALAH (AFTEE) MEELOON PANDA

5. THEN PEENETE POTE KRASEE MESA STOH NOSO-
   KOMEEOH

The answers are:

1. THE CATS DRINK WATER AND MILK BUT THE
   THIEVES DRINK COFFEE

2. THE GIRLS RUN UNDER THE STAIRCASE AND ON THE
   TABLES

3. THE WOMEN MAKE BEAUTIFUL SOUPS BUT THEY
   DON'T MAKE GOOD BEER

4. THE MEN DON'T SPEAK BEFORE THE WOMEN BUT
   THEY ALWAYS SPEAK

5. YOU NEVER DRINK WINE INSIDE THE HOSPITAL

Now cover up the answers below and translate the following:

(You can write your answers in)

1. THESE BOYS DON'T DRINK MILK BUT THE GIRLS DRINK BEER

2. YOU NEVER RUN IN THE ROOM BUT YOU RUN ON THE BEACH

3. YOU ALWAYS MAKE CAKES BUT YOU NEVER MAKE ICE CREAM

4. THEY SPEAK AFTER THEIR FATHER BUT THEY SPEAK BEFORE THEIR MOTHER

5. DO YOU ALWAYS DRINK TEA, AND WHY DON'T YOU SPEAK IMMEDIATELY?

The answers are:

1. AFTAH TA ARROHRYA THEN PEENOON RRALA ALAH TA KOREETSYA PEENOON BEERA

2. THEN TRECHETE POTEH MESA STEEN KAMARA ALAH TRECHETE PANOH STEEN AMOOTHYA

3. KANETE PANDA RRLEEKA ALAH THEN KANETE POTEH PARROTOH

4. AFTEE (AFTES) MEELOON META APOH TON PATERA TOOS ALAH MEELOON PREEN APOH TEEN MEETERA TOOS

5. PEENETE PANDA TSAEE, KEH YATEE THEN MEE-LATE AMESSOS?

ELEMENTARY GRAMMAR

To say	I WANT A DOG
you say	THELO ENA SKEELO
To say	I WANT A BEER
you say	THELO MEEA BEERA
To say	I WANT A FISH
you say	THELO ENA PSAREE

In other words for masculine and neuter words, the word for A is
ENA. For feminine words, the word for A is MEEA.

Now cover up the answers below and translate the following:

(You can write your answers in)

1. AFTEE TROEE MEEA KARTHYA, ENA STOMACHEE KEE ENA LEMO

2. KANO ENA RRLEEKOH KEE ENA FARMAKOH

3. AFTOS PEENEE MEEA BEERA ALAH THEN PEENEE MEEA SOKOLATA

4. AFTEE VLEEPOON ENA ARROHREE KEE ENA BLE BOOKALEE

5. AFTOH THELEE MEEA PETSETA ALAH THEN THELEE ENA PRASEENOH PAPOOTSEE

The answers are:

1. SHE EATS A HEART, A STOMACH AND A NECK

2. I MAKE A CAKE AND A MEDICINE

3. HE DRINKS A BEER BUT HE DOESN'T DRINK A CHOCOLATE

4. THEY SEE A BOY AND A BLUE BOTTLE

5. IT WANTS A TOWEL BUT IT DOESN'T WANT A GREEN SHOE

Now cover up the answers below and translate the following:

(You can write your answers in)

1. I HAVE A FACE AND A PILL
2. YOU SEE A HAND BUT YOU WANT A LEG
3. SHE HAS AN ARM BUT SHE DOESN'T HAVE AN EYE
4. SHE EATS A CAT, A BANANA AND A SALAD
5. I WANT A TELEPHONE AND A DOCTOR

The answers are:

1. ECHO ENA PROSOPOH KEE ENA HAPEE
2. VLEPETE ENA HEAIREE ALAH THELETE ENA POTHEE
3. AFTEE ECHEE ENA BRATSOH ALAH THEN ECHEE ENA MATEE
4. AFTEE TROEE MEEA RRATA, MEEA BANANA KEH MEEA SALATA
5. THELO ENA TEELEFONO KEE ENA YATRO

Section 11 LEARNING THE GREEK ALPHABET

In this last section we will give you the correct pronunciation of the Greek alphabet, so that you will be able to read in Greek. This will apply to capital letters only, at first.

As you may know, the Greek alphabet is quite similar to the English one. There are some letters that look different though and some letters that look the same but which are pronounced differently.

This is the Greek alphabet.

A   B   Γ   Δ   E   Z   H   Θ   I   K   Λ   M

N   Ξ   O   Π   P   Σ   T   Y   Φ   X   Ψ   Ω

We will now teach you the sound of Greek letters with the help of memory aids. They will not be taught in the order above, but in the order best suited to learning the sound of each letter.

1. The Greek letter Γ sounds like rr*
   Imagine Γ looks like a little r
   (* Note: The sound is soft and is a cross between a g, gh and r sound and sometimes sounds like y)
   So rrata (cat) is Γata.

2. The Greek letter Δ sounds like th (in *th*e)
   Imagine Δ is *th*e shape of *th*e pyramids
   So chtapothee (octopus) is chtapoΔee

3. The Greek letter Θ sounds like "th" (in *th*eatre)
   Imagine Θ looks like the circular stage of a *th*eatre
   So thalassa (sea) is Θalassa

4. The Greek letter Λ sounds like "L"
   Imagine Λ looks Like an upside down v – sideways on
   So leemnee (lake) is Λ eemnee

5. The Greek letter Ξ sounds like x
   Imagine three lines are an e*x*tra letter
   (sometimes written as "ks" in the course)
   So exoh (out) is eΞoh

YOU CAN WRITE YOUR ANSWERS IN

What do the following letters sound like?

1. Ξ   _____

2. Λ   _____

3. Θ   _____

4. Δ   _____

5. Γ   _____

TURN BACK FOR THE ANSWERS

Now translate the following into English:

1. toh aⲅoree eenah meⲅaΛoⲎ
2. toh Ξeroh aenΔroh eenah eΔoh
3. ee petaΛooΔa eenah eΞoh
4. toh ⲅala kee toh ⲅrama Δen eenah eΔoh

The answers are:

1. THE BOY IS BIG
2. THE DRY TREE IS HERE
3. THE BUTTERFLY IS OUTSIDE
4. THE MILK AND THE LETTER ARE NOT HERE

THE NEXT SET OF LETTERS

1. The Greek letter Π sounds like p
   Imagine Π looks like a prison window
   So polee (much) is Πolee

2. The Greek letter Σ sounds like s (in *s*ea)
   Imagine Σ is the shape of the *s*ea on a beach
   So soopa (soup) is Σoopa

3. The Greek letter Φ sounds like f
   Imagine Φ looks like a *f*loat on a *f*ishing line
   So feethee (snake) is Φeethee

4. The Greek letter Ψ sounds like the *ps* in ti*psy*
   Imagine Ψ looks like a *ps*ychologist's couch
   So psomee (bread) is Ψomee

5. The Greek letter Ω sounds like "o" (in h*o*t)
   Imagine Ω looks like an "o" on a horseshoe
   So proyee (morning) is prΩyee

YOU CAN WRITE YOUR ANSWERS IN

What is the English sound of

1. Ω   _____

2. Ψ   _____ .

3. Φ   _____

4. Σ   _____

5. Π   _____

TURN BACK FOR THE ANSWERS

Now translate the following into English:

1. toh kaφe caΠeΛo eenah eΔΩ
2. oh skeeΛos Δen Πeenee ΓaΛa
3. ee Γata trΩee ΨΩmee
4. oh ariΘmos eekoΣee eenah meΓaΛos
5. oh Φoornos eenah vrΩmeekoΣ

The answers are:

1. THE BROWN HAT IS HERE
2. THE DOG DOESN'T DRINK MILK
3. THE CAT EATS BREAD
4. (THE) NUMBER TWENTY IS BIG
5. THE BAKERY IS DIRTY

THE NEXT SET OF LETTERS

1. The Greek letter B sounds like v
   Imagine you should Be Very strong
   So vlepee (sees) is Blepee

2. The Greek letter H sounds like "ee" (in see)
   Imagine "H" stands for heel
   (the "ee" is very short, almost like the i in lit)
   So kalee (good) is kalH

3. The Greek letter I sounds like "ee" (in see)
   Imagine I am an eel
   (the "ee" is very short, almost like the i in lit)
   So psaree (fish) is psarI

4. The Greek letter P sounds like R
   Imagine you are a PRAT
   So teeree (cheese) is teePee

5. The Greek letter Y sounds like "ee" (in see)
   Imagine you see the sea
   (the "ee" is very short, almost like the i in lit)
   So keema (wave) is kYma

6. The Greek letter X sounds like "h" in heater
   Imagine x marks the spot where I hit you
   So echo (I have) is eXo

Note: "X" also sounds like the CH in LOCH and is sometimes pronounced like the H in HUE.

YOU CAN WRITE YOUR ANSWERS IN

What is the English sound for

1. X   _____

2. Y   _____

3. P   _____

4. I   _____

5. H   _____

6. B   _____

TURN BACK FOR THE ANSWERS

LETTERS THAT SOUND THE SAME IN GREEK AND ENGLISH

The following letters sound the same in English and Greek

A sounds like the A in *A*RMY

E sounds like the E in S*E*T

O sounds like the O in *O*FF

N, T, K, M and Z also sound as they do in English.

Remember that some letters sound different in Greek, but N, O, T, M, A, Z, E, O, K sound the same. So, remember

NOT MAZE OK

These letters are the same in Greek and English.

Now translate the following into English:

1. ΤΟ ΒοοΝΟ eeNah ΨΗΛΟ

2. ΤΑ ΠοοΛΙΑ ΔΕΝ ΤΡΩΝ ΦΡοοΤΑ

3. Η ΜΗΤΕΡΑ ΠΙΝee ΚΡΑΣΙ Κee ΤΡΩee ΤΥΡΙ

4. Η ΣΑΛΑΤΑ ΕΧee ΠΟΛΥ ΛΑΔΙ

5. ΤΟ ΚΑΤΑΣΤΗΜΑ eeNah ΜΕΓΑΛΟ

6. Ο ΠΑΤΕΡΑΣ ΔΕΝ ΤΡΕΧee ΠΟΤΕ

The answers are:

1. THE MOUNTAIN IS HIGH

2. THE BIRDS DON'T EAT FRUITS

3. (THE) MOTHER DRINKS WINE AND EATS CHEESE

4. THE SALAD HAS MUCH OIL

5. THE SHOP IS BIG

6. (THE) FATHER NEVER RUNS

COMBINATIONS OF LETTERS TO PRODUCE CERTAIN SOUNDS

In Greek there are also some combinations of letters, used to produce certain sounds
In the following examples note that we use all the letters you have already been taught:

NT in Greek sounds like d in *d*ay, so:
   domata (tomato) is NTOMATA

ΜΠ in Greek sounds like b in *b*ottle, so
   bookalee (bottle) is ΜΠooΚΑΛΙ

ΓΚ in Greek sounds like g in *g*rey, so
   gree (grey) is ΓΚΡΙ

ΓΓ in Greek sounds like g in *g*rey, so
   agooree (cucumber) is ΑΓΓooΡΙ

YOU CAN WRITE YOUR ANSWERS IN

What is the English sound for

1. ГГ   _____

2. ГК   _____

3. МП   _____

TURN BACK FOR THE ANSWERS

Now translate the following into English

1. ΤΟ ΚΡΑΣΙ eeNah ΜΕΣΑ ΣΤΟ ΜΠοοΚΑΛΙ

2. ΤΟ ΠΟΤΗΡΙ eeNah ΓΚΡΙ

3. ΤΟ ΜΠΛΕ ΧΡΩΜΑ eeNah ΩΡεΟ

4. ΤΑ ΨΑΡΙΑ eeNah ΠΑΝΩ ΣΤΟ ΠΙΑΤΟ

5. Η ΒΑΛΙΤΣΑ eeNah ΜΕΣΑ ΣΤΟ ΠΟΡΤΜΠΑΓΚΑΖ

6. Η ΝΤΟΜΑΤΑ eeNah ΜΕΓΑΛΗ

The answers are:

1. THE WINE IS IN THE BOTTLE

2. THE GLASS IS GREY

3. THE COLOUR BLUE IS BEAUTIFUL

4. THE FISH(ES) ARE ON THE PLATE

5. THE SUITCASE IS IN THE BOOT

6. THE TOMATO IS BIG

MORE COMBINATIONS OF LETTERS TO PRODUCE CERTAIN SOUNDS

Note that in the examples we use all the letters and the combinations you already know.

OY in Greek sounds like OO in BOOK, so
   Bookalee (bottle) is ΜΠΟΥΚΑΛΙ

ΕΙ in Greek sounds like EE in SEE, so
   farmakeeo (chemist's shop) is ΦΑΡΜΑΚΕΙΟ
        (that is, EE is short)

ΟΙ in Greek sounds like EE in SEE, so
   skeelee (dogs) is ΣΚΥΛΟΙ
        (that is, EE is short)

ΑΙ in Greek sounds like E in tEll, so
   macheree (knife) is ΜΑΧΑΙΡΙ

YOU CAN WRITE YOUR ANSWERS IN

What is the English sound for

1. AI   _____

2. OI   _____

3. EI   _____

4. OY   _____

TURN BACK FOR THE ANSWERS

Now translate the following into English:

1. ΟΙ ΒΑΛΙΤΣΕΣ ΕΙΝΑΙ ΠΙΣΩ ΑΠΟ ΤΗΝ ΣΚΑΛΑ
2. Η ΚΑΜΑΡΑ ΜΟΥ ΕΙΝΑΙ ΜΕΓΑΛΗ
3. Η ΑΜΜΟΥΔΙΑ ΔΕΝ ΕΙΝΑΙ ΥΓΡΗ
4. ΤΑ ΠΑΛΙΑ ΜΑΧΑΙΡΙΑ ΕΙΝΑΙ ΜΕΣΑ, ΣΤΟ ΣΥΡΤΑΡΙ
5. ΤΟ ΑΦΕΝΤΙΚΟ ΤΟΥΣ ΕΙΝΑΙ ΜΕΣΑ ΣΤΟ ΤΕΛΩΝΕΙΟ
6. Η ΕΙΣΟΔΟΣ ΕΙΝΑΙ ΕΔΩ

The answers are:

1. THE SUITCASES ARE BEHIND THE STAIRCASE
2. MY ROOM IS BIG
3. THE BEACH IS NOT WET
4. THE OLD KNIVES ARE IN THE DRAWER
5. THEIR BOSS IS INSIDE THE CUSTOMS
6. THE ENTRANCE IS HERE

FINALLY THE LOWER CASE LETTERS ARE AS FOLLOWS:

A	α	–	Lower case looks like an "a"
B	β	–	Looks like a B
Γ	γ	–	Looks like a "y" which is how it is sometimes pronounced
Δ	δ	–	*The* funny shape just has to be learned!
E	ε	–	Looks like a little "E"
Z	ζ	–	Lower case almost an "s" shape – "z"ish in sound!
H	η	–	Both sound like "i" in hint
Θ	θ	–	Both letters look similar
I	ι	–	Big and little I
K	κ	–	Looks similar to the capital
Λ	λ	–	Looks similar to the capital
M	μ	–	Both sounds "m" – perhaps you live with a mum
N	ν	–	Both sound like N – remember the navy
Ξ	ξ	–	Both have three lines
O	ο	–	Look the same
Π	π	–	Look similar
P	ρ	–	Look similar
Σ	σ	–	The small letter looks like a smouldering grenade
T	τ	–	Looks like a small version of T
Y	υ	–	Imagine YoU look a little Ill – both sound like the "i" in ill
Φ	φ	–	Both look similar to each other
X	χ	–	Big and little X
Ψ	ψ	–	Big and little
Ω	ω	–	The lower case could look like an olive – both sound like the "o" in olive

This is the end of the course. We hope you have enjoyed it! Of course words and grammar will not be remembered for ever without revision, but if you look at the book from time to time, you will be surprised at how quickly everything comes back.

When you go abroad, do not be too shy to try out what you have learnt. Your host will appreciate your making the effort to speak, even if you sometimes make mistakes. And the more you attempt to speak the more you will learn!

GLOSSARY

Note: The line underneath the word shows where the stress on the word should be.

English	Greek pronounciation/Greek
a (m)	ena ENA
a (f)	meea MIA
a (n)	ena ENA
accident	thisticheema (n) ΔΥΣΤΥΧΗΜΑ
aeroplane	aeroplanoh ΑΕΡΟΠΛΑΝΟ
after	meta ΜΕΤΑ
also	epeesees ΕΠΙΣΗΣ
always	panda ΠΑΝΤΑ
ambulance	asthenoforoh ΑΣΘΕΝΟΦΟΡΟ
ancient sites	archea (n, plural) ΑΡΧΑΙΑ
and	keh ΚΑΙ or kee ΚΙ
angry	theemo menoh ΘΥΜΩΜΕΝΟ
animal	zawoh ΖΩΟ
apple	meeloh ΜΗΛΟ
are (you)	eesseh ΕΙΣΑΙ
are (we)	eemasteh ΕΙΜΑΣΤΕ
are (they)	eenah ΕΙΝΑΙ
arm	bratsoh ΜΠΡΑΤΣΟ
armchair	poleethrona ΠΟΛΥΘΡΟΝΑ.
arrival	afeeksee (f) ΑΦΙΞΗ
bad	kakoh ΚΑΚΟ
bakery	foornos ΦΟΥΡΝΟΣ
banana	banana ΜΠΑΝΑΝΑ
bank	trapeza ΤΡΑΠΕΖΑ
barber's shop	kooreeoh ΚΟΥΡΕΙΟ
bath	banyoh ΜΠΑΝΙΟ
bathing suit	mahyoh ΜΑΓΙΩ
beach	amoothya ΑΜΜΟΥΔΙΑ
bean	fasolee ΦΑΣΟΛΙ
beautiful	oreoh ΩΡΑΙΟ
bed	krevatee ΚΡΕΒΑΤΙ
bedroom	krevatoh-kamara ΚΡΕΒΑΤΟΚΑΜΑΡΑ
bee	meleesa ΜΕΛΙΣΣΑ
beer	beera ΜΠΥΡΑ
before	preen ΠΡΙΝ
behind	peesoh ΠΙΣΩ
big	merraloh ΜΕΓΑΛΟ
bill	lorraryasmos ΛΟΓΑΡΙΑΣΜΟΣ
bird	poolee ΠΟΥΛΙ

English	Greek pronounciation/Greek
biscuit	biskotoh ΜΠΙΣΚΟΤΟ
black	mavroh ΜΑΥΡΟ
blood	emah (n) ΑΙΜΑ
blouse	blooza ΜΠΛΟΥΖΑ
blue	ble ΜΠΛΕ
boat	plee oh ΠΛΟΙΟ
boil	speeree ΣΠΥΡΙ
bonnet/hood	kapoh ΚΑΠΩ
boot/trunk	port bagaz ΠΟΡΤΜΠΑΓΚΑΖ
boss	afendeekoh ΑΦΕΝΤΙΚΟ
bottle	bookalee ΜΠΟΥΚΑΛΙ
boy	arrohree ΑΓΟΡΙ
brake	french ΦΡΕΝΟ
bread	psomee ΨΩΜΙ
brother	athelfos ΑΔΕΛΦΟΣ
brown	kafe ΚΑΦΕ
but	alah ΑΛΛΑ
but/for	para ΠΑΡΑ
butcher's shop	hasapeekoh ΥΑΣΑΠΙΚΟ
butterfly	petalootha ΠΕΤΑΛΟΥΔΑ
cake	rrleekoh ΓΛΥΚΟ
camp site	camping ΚΑΜΠΙΝΓΚ
car	aftokeeneetoh ΑΥΤΟΚΙΝΗΤΟ
carpet	halee ΧΑΛΙ
carrot	carotoh ΚΑΡΟΤΟ
cash desk	tameeoh ΤΑΜΕΙΟ
castle	castroh ΚΑΣΤΡΟ
cat	rrata ΓΑΤΑ
celery	seleenoh ΣΕΛΙΝΟ
chair	karekla ΚΑΡΕΚΛΑ
cheese	teeree ΤΥΡΙ
chemist's shop	farmakeeoh ΦΑΡΜΑΚΕΙΟ
cheque	epeetayee (f) ΕΠΙΤΑΓΗ
chocolate	sokolata ΣΟΚΟΛΑΤΑ
church	ekleesya ΕΚΚΛΗΣΙΑ
cloakroom	gardaroba ΓΚΑΡΝΤΑΡΟΜΠΑ
clock	roloee ΡΟΛΟΙ
closed	kleestoh ΚΛΕΙΣΤΟ
coach	pullman ΠΟΥΛΜΑΝ
coat	paltoh ΠΑΛΤΟ
coffee	kafes (m) ΚΑΦΕΣ
cold	kreeoh ΚΡΥΟ
colour	chroma (n) ΧΡΩΜΑ
cough	veechas (m) ΒΗΧΑΣ
cream	krema ΚΡΕΜΑ

English	Greek pronounciation/Greek
cucumber	angooree ΑΓΓΟΥΡΙ
curtain	coorteena ΚΟΥΡΤΙΝΑ
customs	teloneeoh ΤΕΛΩΝΕΙΟ
danger	keentheenos ΚΙΝΔΥΝΟΣ
dark	skoteenoh ΣΚΟΤΕΙΝΟ
daughter	koree ΚΟΡΗ
day	mera ΜΕΡΑ
deer	elafee ΕΛΑΦΙ
departure	anachoreesee (f) ΑΝΑΧΩΡΗΣΗ
diarrhoea	the aria ΔΙΑΡΡΟΙΑ
diesel oil	petreleoh ΠΕΤΡΕΛΑΙΟ
dining room	trapezareea ΤΡΑΠΕΖΑΡΙΑ
dirty	vromeekoh ΒΡΩΜΙΚΟ
doctor	yatros ΓΙΑΤΡΟΣ
dog	skeelos ΣΚΥΛΟΣ
door	porta ΠΟΡΤΑ
drawer	sirtaree ΣΥΡΤΑΡΙ
dress	foostanee ΦΟΥΣΤΑΝΙ
drink	peeno ΠΙΝΩ
dry	kseroh ΞΗΡΟ
duck	papya ΠΑΠΙΑ
ear	aftee ΑΦΤΙ
earth	choma (n) ΧΩΜΑ
eats	troee ΤΡΩΕΙ
egg	avrroh ΑΥΓΟ
engine	meechanee (f) ΜΗΧΑΝΗ
entrance	eesothos (f) ΕΙΣΟΔΟΣ
exit	exothos (f) ΕΞΟΔΟΣ
eye	matee ΜΑΤΙ
face	prosopoh ΠΡΟΣΩΠΟ
father	pateras (m) ΠΑΤΕΡΑΣ
female friend	feelee ΦΙΛΗ
figs	seeka ΣΥΚΑ
fillet steak	feeletoh ΦΙΛΕΤΟ
fire	fotya ΦΩΤΙΑ
first	protoh ΠΡΩΤΟ
fish	psaree ΨΑΡΙ
floor	patoma (n) ΠΑΤΩΜΑ
flu	rreepee (f) ΓΡΥΠΠΗ
fly	meeya ΜΥΓΑ
forest	thassos (n) ΔΑΣΟΣ
fork	peeroonee ΠΗΡΟΥΝΙ
from	apoh ΑΠΟ
fruit	frootoh ΦΡΟΥΤΟ
garage	garaz ΓΚΑΡΑΖ

English	Greek pronounciation/Greek
garden	keepos ΚΗΠΟΣ
garlic	skorthoh ΣΚΟΡΔΟ
girl	koreetsee ΚΟΡΙΤΣΙ
glass	poteeree ΠΟΤΗΡΙ
good	kaloh ΚΑΛΟ
goose	hyeena ΧΗΝΑ
grapes	stafeelya ΣΤΑΦΥΛΙΑ
green	praseenoh ΠΡΑΣΙΝΟ
grey	gree ΓΚΡΙ
grocer's shop	bakaleekoh ΜΠΑΚΑΛΙΚΟ
ham	zambon (n) ΖΑΜΠΟΝ
hand	heairee ΧΕΡΙ
has	echee ΕΧΕΙ
hat	kapeloh ΚΑΠΕΛΟ
he	aftos ΑΥΤΟΣ
heart	karthya ΚΑΡΔΙΑ
heat	zestee (f) ΖΕΣΤΗ
help!	voyeetheea! ΒΟΗΘΕΙΑ
hen	kota ΚΟΤΑ
her	tees ΤΗΣ
here	ethoh ΕΔΩ
his	too ΤΟΥ
horn	klaxon ΚΛΑΞΟΝ
horse	alorroh ΑΛΟΓΟ
hospital	nossokomeeoh ΝΟΣΟΚΟΜΕΙΟ
hour	ora ΩΡΑ
how	pos ΠΩΣ
how much	posso ΠΟΣΟ
husband	andras (m) ΑΝΤΡΑΣ
ice cream	parrotoh ΠΑΓΩΤΟ
ignition	meeza ΜΙΖΑ
illness	arostya ΑΡΡΩΣΤΙΑ
immediately	amessos ΑΜΕΣΩΣ
in (side)	mesa ΜΕΣΑ
insect	endomoh ΕΝΤΟΜΟ
is	eenah ΕΙΝΑΙ
it	aftoh ΑΥΤΟ
its	too ΤΟΥ
jack	rreelos ΓΡΥΛΟΣ
jacket	zaketa ΖΑΚΕΤΑ | ΣΑΚΟΣ
jellyfish	methoosa ΜΕΔΟΥΣΑ
job (work)	thoolya ΔΟΥΛΕΙΑ
jumper (pullover)	poolover ΠΟΥΛΟΒΕΡ
kiosk	pereepteroh ΠΕΡΙΠΤΕΡΟ
kitchen	koozeena ΚΟΥΖΙΝΑ

English	Greek pronounciation/Greek
knife	mach<u>ee</u>ree MAXAIPI
ladies hairdresser	komot<u>ee</u>r<u>ee</u>ooh KOMMΩTHPIO
lake	limn<u>ee</u> (f) ΛIMNH
lamb	arn<u>ee</u> APNI
last	tel<u>ef</u>teoh TEΛEYTAIO
launderette	pleend<u>ee</u>r<u>ee</u>ooh ΠΛYNTHPIO
leg	p<u>othee</u> ΠOΔI
lemonade	lemon<u>a</u>tha ΛEMONAΔA
letter	rr-r<u>ama</u> (n) ΓPAMMA
lettuce	mar<u>oo</u>lee MAPOYΛI
lobster	astak<u>os</u> AΣTAKOΣ
make	k<u>a</u>no KANΩ
male friend	f<u>ee</u>los, ΦIΛOΣ
map	hart<u>ee</u>s XAPTHΣ
market	arr<u>o</u>ra AΓOPA
meat	kr<u>ea</u>s (n) KPEAΣ
medicine	farmak<u>oh</u> ΦAPMAKO
melon	pep<u>o</u>nee ΠEΠONI
menu	men<u>u</u> (n) MENOY
midday	mess<u>ee</u>meree MEΣHMEPI
middle	mess<u>e</u>hoh MEΣAIO
midnight	mess<u>a</u>nichta MEΣANYXTA
milk	rr<u>a</u>la (n) ΓAΛA
minute	lept<u>oh</u> ΛEΠTO
money	left<u>a</u> (n plural) ΛEΦTA
month	m<u>ee</u>nas (n) MHNAΣ
more	pee<u>oh</u> pol<u>ee</u> ΠIO ΠOΛY
morning	proy<u>ee</u> ΠPΩI
mosquito	koon<u>oo</u>pee KOYNOYΠI
mother	meet<u>e</u>ra MHTEPA
mountain	voon<u>oh</u> BOYNO
mouth	st<u>o</u>ma (n) ΣTOMA
much	pol<u>ee</u> ΠOΛY
museum	moss<u>ee</u>ooh MOYΣEIO
my	moo M<u>O</u>Y
name	on<u>o</u>ma (n) ONOMA
neck	l<u>ee</u>mos ΛAIMOΣ
never	pot<u>eh</u> ΠOTE
night	n<u>i</u>chta NYXTA
no	<u>o</u>chee OXI
nose	m<u>ee</u>tee (f) MYTH
not	then ΔEN
number	arithm<u>o</u>s APIΘMOΣ
octopus	chtap<u>othee</u> XTAΠOΔI
office	rr-raf<u>ee</u>ooh ΓPAΦEIO

English	Greek pronounciation/Greek
oil	lathee ΛΑΔΙ
old	palyoh ΠΑΛΙΟ
olive	elya ΕΛΙΑ
on	panoh ΠΑΝΩ
onion	kremeethee ΚΡΕΜΜΥΔΙ
only	monoh ΜΟΝΟ
open	aneechtoh ΑΝΟΙΧΤΟ
or	ee Η
organisation	or-rranosee ΟΡΓΑΝΩΣΗ
our	mas ΜΑΣ
out(side)	exoh ΕΞΩ
pain	ponos ΠΟΝΟΣ
palace	palatee ΠΑΛΑΤΙ
paper	hartee ΧΑΡΤΙ
passport	theeavateereeoh ΔΙΑΒΑΤΗΡΙΟ
pea	arakas (m) ΑΡΑΚΑΣ
pen	steeloh ΣΤΥΛΟ
petrol	venzeenee ΒΕΝΖΙΝΗ
piano	pianoh ΠΙΑΝΟ
picnic	picnic (n) ΠΙΚΝΙΚ
pill	hapee ΧΑΠΙ
plant	feetoh ΦΥΤΟ
plaster	hanzaplast ΧΑΝΖΑΠΛΑΣΤ
plate	piatoh ΠΙΑΤΟ
police	astinomeea ΑΣΤΥΝΟΜΙΑ
pork	heereenoh ΧΟΙΡΙΝΟ
postcard	karta ΚΑΡΤΑ
potato	patata ΠΑΤΑΤΑ
quiet	eeseehoh ΗΣΥΧΟ
rabbit	koonelee ΚΟΥΝΕΛΙ
rain	vrochee (f) ΒΡΟΧΗ
red	kokeenoh ΚΟΚΚΙΝΟ
restaurant	restoran (n) ΡΕΣΤΩΡΑΝ
rice	reezee ΡΥΖΙ
right (correct)	sostoh ΣΩΣΤΟ
river	potamee ΠΟΤΑΜΙ
room	kamara ΚΑΜΑΡΑ
run	trecho ΤΡΕΧΩ
salad	salata ΣΑΛΑΤΑ
salary	misthos ΜΙΣΘΟΣ
salesman	poleetees (m) ΠΩΛΗΤΗΣ
salmon	solomos ΣΟΛΩΜΟΣ
sand	amos (f) ΑΜΜΟΣ
sea	thalassa ΘΑΛΑΣΣΑ
second	thefteroh ΔΕΥΤΕΡΟ

English	Greek pronounciation/Greek
sees	vlepee ΒΛΕΠΕΙ
she	aftee ΑΥΤΗ
shelf	rafee ΠΑΦΙ
shoe	papootsee ΠΑΠΟΥΤΣΙ
shop	katasteema (n) ΚΑΤΑΣΤΗΜΑ
sister	athelfee ΑΔΕΛΦΗ
skirt	foosta ΦΟΥΣΤΑ
small	mikroh ΜΙΚΡΟ
snake	feethee ΦΙΔΙ
soft	malakoh ΜΑΛΑΚΟ
son	yos ΓΙΟΣ
soup	soopa ΣΟΥΠΑ
speak	meelo ΜΙΛΩ
spinach	spanakee ΣΠΑΝΑΚΙ
spoon	cootalee ΚΟΥΤΑΛΙ
staircase	scala ΣΚΑΛΑ
starter	mezes (m) ΜΕΖΕΣ
steering wheel	teemonee ΤΙΜΟΝΙ
sting	tseembeema (n) ΤΣΙΜΠΗΜΑ
stomach	stomachee ΣΤΟΜΑΧΙ
street	othos (f) ΟΔΟΣ
stupid	hazoh ΧΑΖΟ
sugar	zacharee ΖΑΧΑΡΗ
suitcase	valeetsa ΒΑΛΙΤΣΑ
sun	eelyos ΗΛΙΟΣ
supermarket	supermarket ΣΟΥΠΕΡΜΑΡΚΕΤ
sweet	rrleekoh ΓΛΥΚΟ
table	trapezee ΤΡΑΠΕΖΙ
tall	pseeloh ΨΗΛΟ
tank	depozitoh ΝΤΕΠΟΖΙΤΟ
tea	tsaee ΤΣΑΪ
telephone	telefonoh ΤΗΛΕΦΩΝΟ
temple	naos ΝΑΟΣ
tent	skinee (f) ΣΚΗΝΗ
the (m) (subject)	oh Ο
the (f) (subject)	ee Η
the (n) (subject)	toh ΤΟ
their	toos ΤΟΥΣ
there	ekee ΕΚΕΙ
they (f)	aftes ΑΥΤΕΣ
they (m)	aftee ΑΥΤΟΙ
they (n)	aftah ΑΥΤΑ
thief	kleftees (m) ΚΛΕΦΤΗΣ
thin	leptoh ΛΕΠΤΟ
ticket	eeseeteereeoh ΕΙΣΙΤΗΡΙΟ

English	Greek pronounciation/Greek
tide	paleerya ΠΑΛΙΡΡΟΙΑ
tin can	konserva ΚΟΝΣΕΡΒΑ
today	seemera ΣΗΜΕΡΑ
toilet	tooaleta ΤΟΥΑΛΕΤΑ
tomato	domata ΝΤΟΜΑΤΑ
tooth	thondee ΔΟΝΤΙ
tortoise	helona ΧΕΛΩΝΑ
towel	petseta ΠΕΤΣΕΤΑ
train	trenoh ΤΡΑΙΝΟ
tree	thendroh ΔΕΝΤΡΟ
trousers	pantelonee ΠΑΝΤΕΛΟΝΙ
tuna fish	tonos ΤΟΝΝΟΣ
tyre	lasticho ΛΑΣΤΙΧΟ
under	catoh ΚΑΤΩ
veal	moscharee ΜΟΣΧΑΡΙ
very	polee ΠΟΛΥ
vinegar	xithee ΞΥΔΙ
waiter	garsonee ΓΚΑΡΣΟΝΙ
wall	teechos ΤΟΙΧΟΣ
wants	thelee ΘΕΛΕΙ
was	eetan ΗΤΑΝ
wasp	sfeeka ΣΦΗΚΑ
water	neroh ΝΕΡΟ
wave	keema (n) ΚΥΜΑ
week	evthomatha ΕΒΔΟΜΑΔΑ
wet	eerr-roh ΥΓΡΟ
wheel	trochos ΤΡΟΧΟΣ
when	pote ΠΟΤΕ
where	poo ΠΟΥ
white	asproh ΑΣΠΡΟ
why	yatee ΓΙΑΤΙ
wife	yeeneka ΓΥΝΑΙΚΑ
wine	krasee ΚΡΑΣΙ
wolf	leekos ΛΥΚΟΣ
worm	skooleekee ΣΚΟΥΛΗΚΙ
wrong	lathos (n) ΛΑΘΟΣ
year	chronos ΧΡΟΝΟΣ
yes	neh ΝΑΙ
yesterday	chthes ΧΘΕΣ
young	neoh ΝΕΟ
your (plural)	sas ΣΑΣ
your (singular)	soo ΣΟΥ

Numbers

zero	meethen ΜΗΔΕΝ

Numbers

one	ena	ΕΝΑ
two	theeoh	ΔΥΟ
three	treea	ΤΡΙΑ
four	teresa	ΤΕΣΣΕΡΑ
five	pende	ΠΕΝΤΕ
six	exee	ΕΞΙ
seven	efta	ΕΦΤΑ
eight	ochtoh	ΟΧΤΩ
nine	enya	ΕΝΝΙΑ
ten	theka	ΔΕΚΑ
eleven	entheka	ΕΝΔΕΚΑ
twelve	thotheka	ΔΩΔΕΚΑ
twenty	eekossee	ΕΙΚΟΣΙ
twenty-five	eekossee pende	ΕΙΚΟΣΙ ΠΕΝΤΕ

Days of the week

Monday	theftera	ΔΕΥΤΕΡΑ
Tuesday	treetee	ΤΡΙΤΗ
Wednesday	tetartee	ΤΕΤΑΡΤΗ
Thursday	pemtee	ΠΕΜΠΤΗ
Friday	paraskevee	ΠΑΡΑΣΚΕΥΗ
Saturday	savatoh	ΣΑΒΒΑΤΟ
Sunday	keeryakee	ΚΥΡΙΑΚΗ

LINKWORD AUDIO TAPES

An audio tape is available as an extra learning aid to accompany this book.

It allows you to hear and to practise the correct pronunciation for all the words used on this course.

The tape is available by mail order using the order form at the back of this book.

Other LINKWORD AUDIO TAPES:

0 552 13225X   French
0 552 132268   German
0 552 132276   Spanish
0 552 132284   Italian
0 552 139661   Portuguese

LINKWORD BOOK AND AUDIO TAPE PACKS

The following LINKWORD courses are also available in packs combining the books with the relevant pronunciation cassette tape.

These are available either by mail order, using the form at the back of this book, or you can buy the pack from any good bookshop:

0 552 139572   French
0 552 139599   Spanish

LINKWORD ON COMPUTER

First Courses
*FRENCH *GERMAN *SPANISH *ITALIAN
*GREEK *RUSSIAN *DUTCH *PORTUGUESE

On IBM PC & COMPATIBLES, APPLE II Series,
MACINTOSH and COMMODORE 64

GCSE LEVEL FRENCH

An extensive vocabulary and grammar up to GCSE level
standard, ideal as a follow-up course to the book or first
course programs or as a revision or "brush-up" course for the
rusty!

Available on IBM PC & Compatibles.

All courses available from

U.S.A.

ARTWORX INC.,
1844 PENFIELD ROAD,
PENFIELD,
NEW YORK.
TEL: (716) 385 6120

LINKWORD LANGUAGE SYSTEM BOOKS, AUDIO TAPES AND BOOK AND TAPE PACKS AVAILABLE FROM CORGI BOOKS

13053 2	LINKWORD LANGUAGE SYSTEM: FRENCH	£4.99
13054 0	LINKWORD LANGUAGE SYSTEM: GERMAN	£4.99
13055 9	LINKWORD LANGUAGE SYSTEM: SPANISH	£4.99
13056 7	LINKWORD LANGUAGE SYSTEM: ITALIAN	£4.99
13907 6	LINKWORD LANGUAGE SYSTEM: GREEK	£4.99
13906 8	LINKWORD LANGUAGE SYSTEM: PORTUGUESE	£4.99
13225 X	LINKWORD AUDIO TAPE: FRENCH	£6.95
13226 8	LINKWORD AUDIO TAPE: GERMAN	£6.95
13227 6	LINKWORD AUDIO TAPE: SPANISH	£6.95
13228 4	LINKWORD AUDIO TAPE: ITALIAN	£6.95
13955 6	LINKWORD AUDIO TAPE: GREEK	£6.95
13966 1	LINKWORD AUDIO TAPE: PORTUGUESE	£6.95
13957 2	LINKWORD BOOK AND TAPE PACK: FRENCH	£9.99
13959 9	LINKWORD BOOK AND TAPE PACK: SPANISH	£9.99